MANAGERIAL
DEVIANCE

MANAGERIAL DEVIANCE

HOW TO DEAL WITH PROBLEM PEOPLE IN KEY JOBS

ANDREW J. DUBRIN

 MASON/CHARTER

NEW YORK 1976

658.3
D 819M

Library of Congress Cataloging in Publication Data

DuBrin, Andrew J
    Managerial deviance.

    Includes index.
    1. Executives. 2. Executives--Psychology.
3. Deviant behavior. 4. Personnel management.
I. Title.
HF5500.2.D8   658.3   76-971
ISBN 0-88405-134-X

Once again to Drew and Douglas
and now also to Melanie

Contents

Preface

Deviant behavior among members of management, both in business and government, has received widespread public attention in the early and middle 1970s. Several types of deviant behavior in management have long been considered to lie outside of tolerable limits. Embezzlers, corporate espionage agents ("industrial spies"), blackmailers, arsonists, and a variety of other criminal types are universally considered people unfit to hold key positions in work organizations who rely on the public for support. If discovered, criminals have always been forcibly invited to leave such organizations as General Motors, city governments, or the local high school.

Another general category of deviants have been considered unfit to occupy leadership positions in work organizations—those suffering from full-blown mental illnesses. A company president unable to concentrate on his work and whose memory for recent events has all but disappeared is usually asked to accept medical retirement. The local governmental official whose suspicious nature finally blossoms into paranoid delusions about people in other departments is usually shunted in the direction of immediate psychiatric consultation. His return to office is contingent upon some form of medical release which suggests that his paranoid ideation is now contained.

Another group of managers and staff people exhibit job-related behavior that deviates below the acceptable minimum standards an organization can tolerate. Some people are grossly ineffective in their occupational roles, stemming from a lack of training, experience, or aptitude for their work. Thousands of victims of the Peter Principle are unable to make a positive contribution to their organizations because they have been promoted into positions which lie beyond their capabilities.

Managerial deviancy deals with a small proportion of people in management whose aberrant behavior has a disproportionate negative impact on the organization, yet who are not criminals, psychotics, simple neurotics, or outright misfits in their jobs. *Managerial deviants* are those management-level workers (generally males and occasionally a female) whose maladaptive behavior stems from some variety of character disorder or personality disturbance. Included here are pathological liars, manipulaters, alcoholics, drug abusers, sexual exploiters of subordinates, and blatant abusers of power.

Describing managerial deviancy, however, is not sufficient to justify writing an entire book. My experience as a consultant and author of behavioral science-based books suggests that the world wants prescription along with description. No managerial psychologist with professional integrity would suggest that behavioral science has arrived at a definitive technology for eliminating aberrant behavior in management, but plenty of useful information is ready for application. In short, *Managerial Deviance* represents both a game plan and a strategy for dealing with aberrant behavior in management. Ideally, following the prescriptions in this book will redirect the energies of many deviants early in their careers, before their aberrant behavior has cancerous consequences for themselves and the organizations in which they work.

Acknowledgments

A number of people helped me with this project. Henry A. Paasonen receives my primary thanks for urging me to write a book about deviant behavior in management. Nancy Davis, my editor at Mason/Charter, commandeered the manuscript through its production and promotion stages, while simultaneously boosting my morale with her enthusiasm. Marcia R. DuBrin, my confidante, fan, life partner, and wife, receives my thanks for her keen interest in my writing and research.

K. Lois Smith performed in her usual superior manner as my manuscript typist—a vital contribution. Students of mine in the Master of Business Administration program at R.I.T. served as careful observers of the aberrant behavior of others, thus providing many case examples of managerial deviance. Professor Sang M. Lee provided several important editorial and technical suggestions which were incorporated in the revision of the manuscript.

Most of the case histories and case examples reported in this book (unless otherwise indicated) stem from direct and indirect observations in a variety of organizations. Many examples presented are an amalgam of two or more situations. Due to the sensitive nature of deviant behavior in work organizations, all case examples have been carefully disguised.

Andrew J. DuBrin

March 3, 1976
Rochester, New York

1

Meet the Deviant Managers

"How did that incompetent ever become an executive? Why doesn't somebody do something to get rid of him before he does any more damage?" Sentiments such as these are quietly expressed in the corridors, cafeterias, and washrooms of countless organizations, about that small proportion of executives who exhibit deviant behavior in the conduct of their normal work. Stockholders, members of the board of directors, and immediate superiors are frequently the last to realize that a member of the management team is engaging in aberrant behavior. Even the most deviant managers usually retain enough rational behavior to appear competent when interacting with their immediate superiors or the public. Subordinates of ineffective, amoral, corrupt, and/or subcriminal managers are assigned the unenviable chore of suffering under their leadership.

Deviant behavior at the highest administrative levels received widespread public attention in the early 1970s with the investigations of Watergate, Equity Funding, and International Telephone and Telegraph. Deviance on such a grand scale only dramatized what has been known about multilayered organizations (and some small family businesses) for many years. For a variety of complex reasons, a

1

small proportion of people in key positions exhibit behavior that unequivocally deviates from what common sense and prudent judgment would consider acceptable, constructive, purposive behavior. According to estimates made in a wide variety of organizations by several different researchers, it is safe to conclude that anywhere from 5 to 15 percent of managers and top-level staff people exhibit deviant behavior *during working hours.*[1]

Managerial deviance, according to the philosophical and psychological position taken here, is *maladaptive behavior in a managerial-level worker, stemming from a personality, character, or value defect that has an adverse impact on an organization, both in terms of job performance and/or morale.* An ineffective individual is not necessarily a managerial deviant; his or her deviance may stem from a variety of factors that have little to do with personality, character, or values. A person who exhibits deviant behavior on his or her own time without that behavior having an adverse effect on job performance is not a managerial deviant. Weekend drug abusers or alcoholics who recuperate completely by Monday (a rare phenomenon) are not managerial deviants. An account executive with nymphomaniacal tendencies who confines her sexual excesses to after-work hours (and an occasional long lunch) is also not a managerial deviant. Before examining some case histories of managerial deviants, it is necessary to mention a variety of other problem people sometimes found in management who are not managerial deviants.

Managers suffering from brain disorders because of problems such as head injuries, cerebral arteriosclerosis, or high fevers may be ineffective and occasionally bizarre in their job-related behavior, yet they are not to be classified as managerial deviants. A manager who experiences a transient situational disturbance because his child died in a fire may become ineffective in his work, yet he is not a managerial deviant. People in management and staff positions sometimes develop neurotic or psychotic reaction patterns and therefore become obsolete in their jobs, but their obsolescence cannot be attributed to a personality or value defect. Managers sometimes perform dismally in their jobs because of insufficient intelligence; low mental ability is the nature of their problem, not managerial deviance.

Other managers may fail on the job and lower the morale of others simply because they are misplaced by reason of aptitude, temperament, or training for their current job. A small proportion of people in managerial positions are effective but eccentric. These people are different but not deviant. Finally, outright criminals such as embezzlers, swindlers, and arsonists can also be found in management ranks. Maladaptive behavior of this magnitude similarly lies outside the scope of managerial deviance.

According to our framework, deviant behavior among managerial personnel can only be measured in terms of its consequences to the organization. When an action stemming from a personality, character, or value defect leads to lowered job performance, has a significant negative impact on the morale and/or mental health of other people in the organization, or detracts from organizational goals, only then can it be considered managerial deviance. The weekend transvestite is not a managerial deviant if his weekend preference for wearing woman's clothing does not adversely affect his job performance. However, a personnel director who gets into fist fights at parties in the presence of other company personnel must be considered a managerial deviant. His immature and aggressive behavior during off hours lowers his credibility as a professional person in the area of human relations. Other managers will not bring sensitive issues to his attention because his judgment is suspect.

Among the deviant managers and staff people described or alluded to in this book are alcoholics, sexual exploiters of subordinates, drug abusers, moral deviants, Machiavellians, AWOL executives, management hustlers, pathological liars, con men and women, compulsive gamblers, and abdicators of authority.

Detecting and confronting various forms of managerial deviance is a vital first step in a results-oriented approach to the proper resolution of the problems created by deviant behavior in high places. Some of the specific case examples of managerial deviants will remind the reader of someone in his or her place of work, past or present.

Larry, the Alcoholic Dean

Dr. Larry Martin is the dean of social sciences at a state university, a position he has held for seven years since his promotion from associate dean at a neighboring college. Above all, Larry is likeable and noncontroversial. Handsome and youthful in appearance, Dr. Martin is described by his supporters as "strong in human relations skills" and "sensitive to people." When not directly or indirectly under the effects of alcohol, Larry is also an effective administrator.

A glimpse at Larry Martin's mode of operation helps explain how an alcoholic can continue to function as an academic dean. Dr. Martin has learned well the importance of surrounding himself with capable assistants and delegating substantial responsibility to them. Students and faculty members at his school, for instance, recognize that Larry's administrative secretary provides answers to most minor problems. When a faculty member wants quick approval of a minor travel expenditure, the unofficial word is "Ask Myra; she'll get it approved." Should a student require a class section change because of a personality conflict with a professor, Myra does the appropriate juggling. Another subordinate of Larry's, the associate dean, handles most of the detailed planning functions such as course scheduling and student registrations. Committees are assigned to study all special problems that arise. Larry reviews reports and makes action recommendations during the morning hours. As Larry told a young professor: "I'll discuss your committee report on academic standards with you in the morning. I think better on an empty stomach."

Larry drinks heavily at lunch about three days a week. Myra protects him from visitors on these days by scheduling conferences only between ten and twelve in the morning. Emergency conferences are scheduled between 3:00 and 5:00 P.M. Larry rationalizes that "people can discuss their work concerns best over a drink," which justifies inviting faculty members to join him at a nearby cocktail lounge around five in the afternoon. Conventions and professional meetings allow Larry to feed his alcohol addiction for days at a time. One of Larry's former faculty members describes his social behavior at a convention.

"I must admit, Larry Martin is one swell person to attend a meeting with. He has no intention of listening to presentations and bringing ideas back to the school. All he wants to do is meet people and imbibe. Few people I have met could keep up with Larry's drinking. He invited me to join him for a drink after our three-hour trip to New York. Larry had four martinis in one sitting. I have read novels in which an advertising man has five martinis at lunch, but I never believed that a person could absorb that much alcohol into the bloodstream without becoming comatose. During the three days of meetings, Larry kept on encouraging me to have a few drinks to loosen up a little. Larry's recurring phrase is, 'A person works harder than most people think in academic life. Why not relax while you have the chance?' Despite his almost nonstop drinking, Larry was back in the office Monday morning, chatting with people and telling them what a growth experience the meetings were."

Larry Martin is only one of an estimated four million alcoholics holding full-time jobs. Repeated evidence from several sources suggests that 5 to 8 percent of the work force in the United States has a drinking problem severe enough to classify them as alcoholic.[2] Alcoholism among managers appears to be as frequent (or even more frequent) than among people at lower organization levels. As many as one in every twelve managers is an alcoholic, according to the National Council on Alcoholism. Typically he (and in some cases, she) is between 35 and 54 years old and has been on the job twelve years.

Paradoxically, the symptoms displayed by the alcoholic manager or staff person are precisely those kinds of behavior that interfere with effective performance in managerial or staff work. Most people recognize that a person with an above-average level of alcohol in the blood cannot make accurate mathematical calculations, design bridges, or perform psychosurgery. Managerial work also suffers gravely. Alcoholics show poor judgment, erratic behavior, imprecise

thinking, indecisiveness, and typically miss deadlines because of their frequent absences from work. My observation
is that alcoholic managers contribute only about 10 productive hours per week to their job. The balance of the work
week is spent thinking about drinking, actual drinking, or
recovering from its effects. A back-from-lunch alcoholic
usually requires a 30-minute coffee break to ready himself or
herself to face normal work responsibilities.

Despite the gravity of the problem, the recovery rate for
alcoholic managers is about 70 percent, assuming both the
organization and the alcoholic take a constructive approach
to rehabilitation.[3] Modification of deviant behavior in management, however, is the central message of this book and
will be pursued at length in subsequent chapters.

Clyde, the Sexual Exploiter

Clyde King was the administrative vice-president in the
home office of a medium-size life insurance company.
Recognizing that most company employees were female, yet
career opportunities for them were limited, Clyde initiated a
career development plan for women. According to this new
program, young women who entered the company as file
clerks could move through the steno pool, up into departments, and then into a variety of supervisory and administrative assistant positions.

As coordinator of the program, Clyde had the legitimate
opportunity to periodically visit the steno pool and confer
with the supervisors to discuss the progress of the program.
In the process he also took the chance to observe which en-
trants to the steno pool appeared particularly attractive.
Young women in this category became candidates for
Clyde's unofficial, *accelerated* career development program.

Every three months Clyde gave another girl an opportunity to work as an administrative intern in his office (first clear-
ing the appointment with her supervisor). The intern thus
had the opportunity to acquire an inside view of the major
kinds of administrative decisions faced by the company.

She would also have the chance to participate in a variety of special projects, one of which was designed to improve Clyde's morale and feelings of masculinity. "King's Harem" was apparently in operation for almost two years before an irate employee's comments in an exit interview led to an investigation and Clyde's dismissal. Bev, one of his victims, explains how the unpublicized aspects of the administrative intern program worked.

"Mr. King capitalized on his charm, power, and the naïveté of the girls who were selected for the special intern program. First of all, a 20-year-old girl would have to be awed at the prospects of working in the office of a top company executive. Add to that the fact that suave Clyde fits the Hollywood image of the successful executive. Because he is well dressed, debonair, well mannered, and good-looking, young girls find him very attractive even if he has a wife and children.

"After he got to know you, Mr. King would invite you to lunch and hold no punches about his intentions. He would point out that the company had many ambitious and hardworking young women who wanted to get ahead. He prefered to recommend for promotion those girls he found very agreeable from a personal standpoint, providing, of course, they are also good workers. *Personally agreeable,* in Clyde King's language, meant that you would have an affair with him. Lunch hours were best for Clyde's affairs because they didn't interfere with his home life. He certainly was a gentleman. Champagne or other fine wine and a cute little studio apartment less than 10 blocks from the office. I'll admit that the setting for his sexual encounters with administrative interns was romantic.

"Before I sound as if I'm painting the picture of a patron saint, I have to explain one spicy detail. Having sex with Clyde King usually did more for him than it did for you. He made some vague promises to girls that he really couldn't keep. To give you one specific example, he hinted to several girls separately that they might become the word processing manager if they cooperated with him socially."

How common is the sex exploiter of subordinates? Factual data about the incidence of this type of practice is limited. Trading sex for income and work assignments in the entertainment field is common practice, according to the folklore of Hollywood and New York. Research this author conducted for *Survival in the Sexist Jungle* suggests that sexual exploitation of subordinates is an uncommon but not unheard of practice in corporate life.[4] It is useful to differentiate between the use of prostitutes as customer entertainment and the sexual exploitation of subordinates. The former is a fairly widespread business practice which, however illegal (and immoral from some viewpoints), is an explicit bargain. Sexual favors are bought for customers in order to maintain goodwill. It is a practice that is considered similar to entertaining customers in restaurants or at sporting events.

Sexual exploitation of subordinates usually involves a superior abusing formal power in order to entice a subordinate into a sexual relationship. The person exploited is led to believe that having sex with the exploiter will lead to more responsibility and income. Exploitation comes about when the promise is not fulfilled. Whether or not the promise is fulfilled, formal power has been abused. To complicate the issues further, sexual exploitation of subordinates can take place only when the subordinate in question is willing to engage in a minor form of prostitution in order to advance her (*his* when the person in power is a male homosexual or a female) position or income.

Peter, the Drug Abuser

"Drug-taking is a lot more prevalent than top management is willing to admit," states Eugene Jennings, a widely quoted management psychologist.[5] Peter, the advertising and sales promotion manager of a large commercial printer, represents one case history of a drug-dependent middle manager. Peter entertains the delusion that his creativity and high output can only be sustained with the help of amphetamines. When work pressures mount, he increases his ingestion of "bennies" or "pep pills." At the point of his detection, Peter had increased his intake of amphetamines to 200 milligrams per day, sometimes combining pep pills with alcohol when work pressures were the highest. He had long been observed as "hyper" and "manicky" by his co-workers. When asked by his immediate superior about his surges of energy and restlessness, Peter once replied: "These damn diet pills my doctor prescribed for me tend to rev me up." Peter's drug habit led to his dismissal from the company on the basis of one dramatic incident with a complicated background.

Peter was assigned major responsibility in an advertising campaign designed to cultivate business in a new geographic area for the company. A review of the project at its culmination was scheduled with the management team. One week before this top-management review, Peter's boss made a routine status check of progress on the project. Asked about the illustrations and advertising copy, Peter told his boss: "No sweat, this project is coming home beautifully. Bonnie [a specialist in his department] is now going over things with a fine tooth comb to make sure every detail is correct. This will be one helluva presentation. Just trust the judgment of our department. You can't force creativity. I've never blown a big one yet. Let us surprise you. It will be sensational."

Reluctantly, Peter's boss acceded to his request not to monitor the project further and wait for the presentation. Three days later Peter sent a frantic message to his boss: "Bert, we need a one-week postponement. This project has got to be perfect. Some unavoidable delays have come up in the color rendering of our advertising copy. I don't want to point the finger at any one person, so will you please give us a one-week extension? The integrity of our department is hanging on this campaign. It's a biggie. I'll send you over a sketch of the major thrust of our proposed advertising copy. Okay for now?"

Bert regarded the intermediate product as promising but lacking polish and punch. Using this as an early warning signal that things were not going smoothly on the project, Bert made an impromptu visit to Peter's department at 3:00

P.M. two days before the scheduled presentation. As Bert describes it:

> I have never seen anything quite like that in a business situation before. Peter appeared to have flipped. He was talking away a mile a minute, and his hands were shaking as he shuffled like mad through a pile of papers on his desk. The moment he looked up at me, I could tell something was seriously wrong. His pupils were twice the normal size and he had a glassy-eyed appearance. He took off on a tirade about his artist not being creative. Peter looked like he had been in a street fight. His clothing was disheveled and soaked with perspiration. We called the company doctor who came over in a half hour and gave Peter a sedative to combat his overdose of uppers. Peter was put on a medical leave of absence for two weeks and then let go with two months severance pay. I wish we had got to him earlier.

Drug abuse among managerial personnel is generally confined to heavy reliance on marijuana, with the overuse of amphetamines and sedatives running a close second.[6] Hard drugs such as heroin, cocaine, LSD, and mescaline are much less frequently used by staff and management people, but they still constitute an ominous problem. To illustrate, a recent National Institute of Mental Health survey of 34,000 employed heroin addicts revealed that 9.8 percent are professionals, technical workers, managers, and owners.[7] Equally alarming, a survey of 227,000 employed, habitual users of barbiturates and other sedatives revealed that 23.8 percent were professionals, technical workers, managers, and owners.[8] An unknown proportion of these drug addicts abscond with company funds or merchandise to support their habit.

Tony, the Moral Deviant

Tony, the president of a small pharmaceutical company, is heavily concerned about morality in the drug business.

All the products of his company meet or exceed government safety standards for the testing of drugs before placing them on the market. He is also moralistic about ecology. Tony's company adds to the beauty of the industrial park in which it is located. The emission from company smokestacks is considered safe by ecological standards. Tony's brand of immorality manifests itself in his attitude toward people over 50. In a conference with his personnel director, Tony suggests a new, informal policy for his company:

> I'm concerned about our image in this company. _____ Pharmaceutical is a young dynamic company, going places in a competitive field. We want to attract youthful, vigorous people. I think one reason holding us back from getting the youthful people we want at all ranks in the company is the age of most of our current employees. Look around and you will see what I mean. As you walk in the door, you see a receptionist in her forties. Unheard of in a glamorous company. Most of the first-line supervisors are in their late forties or early fifties. Few young people want to work for members of the older generation. What about getting more of those young, attractive mod types into our laboratory?
>
> My plan is to start phasing out some of the older supervisors and workers. Encourage them to retire in a graceful way. Don't put anybody new into a public contact or supervisory position who is over 35. If you dare write an official memo on this subject, I will deny that it was my suggestion. This is something we are going to do without a lot of fanfare. We don't want an investigation by the State Employment Commission.

Tony is more strident in his views than most moral deviants who practice job discrimination against people because of their age, sex, race, or religion; yet age discrimination is a national problem. Ms. Carin Ann Clauss, associate solicitor of the United States Fair Labor Standards Division, notes: "Age discrimination is the most illusive and damaging type of discrimination. It cuts down workers in their prime."[9] Congress passed the age discrimination law in 1968. Since

then approximately 7,000 Labor Department investigations
reveal that white-collar workers, especially members of middle and upper management, are the most frequent victims of
age discrimination. Next are unskilled laborers. Least affected are employees with valuable mechanical and technical
skills who receive union protection.

Roger, the Machiavellian

A pure Machiavellian is characterized by "an amoral, manipulative attitude toward other individuals, combined with
a cynical view of man's motives and of their character."[10]
Roger Crowell, the former director of a management consulting firm and onetime executive in a chemical company,
fits this description. Crowell's consulting firm was beset
with problems of low morale, high turnover, and frequent
disputes among its various divisions about the allocation of
personnel and resources. His Machiavellian attitude toward
running a professional organization apparently contributed
to these problems. Roger's manipulative, politically orient-
ed approach to organizational life is illustrated in this sampling of his behavior:

> Roger Crowell, the president, was especially sensitive
> to the image he portrayed to present and/or potential cli-
> ents, and to personnel below him in the organization.
> When a visitor to the firm presented himself at the re-
> ception desk, he was asked to be seated and told, "Mr.
> Crowell will be with you shortly." Within several min-
> utes the visitor would be escorted to a small anteroom
> outside Crowell's office. Here the visitor was usually re-
> quired to wait fifteen minutes before he could be seen
> by the president. Asked by an internal staff member
> why he used the anteroom, Crowell responded,
> ". . . To create the right impression of a dynamic,
> busy, consulting firm."
> Crowell employed another tactic to impress both out-
> siders and internal personnel. Conversations with visi-

tors to his office were frequently interrupted by a buzz from his secretary. He would ritualistically pick up the phone, cup the receiver in his hand, and announce, "Excuse me, this is from Los Angeles" (the city would change from time to time). Soon it became well documented that the secretary was instructed to fabricate these phone calls. Part of Crowell's responsibility as president was to attract new business to the firm. During staff meetings he would report on the status of client development activities. At three consecutive staff meetings he made the point that although a particular company was ". . . quite interested in our firm working with them, I am not sure that theirs is the kind of problem we want to undertake." Staff members recognized that new business prospects were slim and that Crowell was either rationalizing or lying.[11]

Machiavellianism and other forms of political maneuvering constitute a widespread form of managerial deviance in both large and small organizations. Resources are misallocated and time and money are wasted as managerial personnel at all levels carry out their struggles for career advancement and the acquisition of power. The palace revolt at Ford Motor Company in 1970 is a legendary example of the struggle for power within hierarchical organizations.[12] Simon E. Knudsen was brought to Ford as president after having served in a top management position with General Motors. After less than two years at Ford he was fired, largely because he was unable to form an alliance with the powerful Lee Iacocca.

Vance, the AWOL Middle Manager

Vance, manager of consumer services at First National Trust Company, has diverse recreational interests. During a recent month Vance saw three afternoon baseball games, attended four art shows, went bowling twice, had his hair styled, was outfitted for a custom suit of clothing, and attended three sessions of a speed reading class. None of these activities subtracted anything from Vance's family life— they were all accomplished during normal bank working hours. After several months of being AWOL, Vance felt guilty and frustrated about his lack of contribution and wanted to find productive employment. Conducting his job-hunting campaign on company time, he found a job on the marketing staff of a smaller bank where his contribution was needed and his work could be measured.

During the corporate belt-tightening period of approximately 1969 to 1974, AWOLism among management became less prevalent. Many business and nonprofit organizations decreased their number of middle managers, yet the workload either remained constant or actually increased. With "more work to do and fewer people to do it," a commonplace phenomenon, absenteeism in the ranks of management could be more readily detected. Nevertheless, the absentee manager is yet another form of managerial deviance.[13] Vance explains how his organization created an environment in which AWOLism could be practiced by managers:

Somehow our bank management never took seriously new developments in managing people. Even a first-year business student would have a better approach to managing people than did the top executives in our bank. Our president was a strong advocate of autocratic management and unilateral decision making. I was appointed the manager of customer services because professional banking associations are now saying that banks have to be nice to customers—just like supermarkets or restaurants. With branches of other banks and now even some foreign banks proliferating in large numbers, banking has become a competitive business. The job of our department was to find ways to improve customer service and attract new business.

You probably think this sounded like an ideal opportunity, being a marketing manager in a good-sized trust company. It could have been if top management would

have let me do my job. Working with a staff of three people, we began to generate some really creative ideas,
such as putting a branch in a large suburban supermar-
ket. But the president would hardly even acknowledge
my memos and reports. An ecstatic statement from him
was 'This report certainly has merit. I intend to give it
further thought.' Here I was heading up a small group
generating reports and recommendations that were
probably not going to be used. Our president thought
customer services consisted mostly of giving away electric blankets to new depositers.

After a couple of months of this organized futility, I
began to take long lunch hours. Then I began to realize
that it really didn't matter if I came back from lunch at
all. Soon my absences from the office became kind of
addictive. I found myself taking care of miscellaneous
errands on company time, such as having a will prepared, getting an eye examination for my operator's license, gift shopping, and having my shoes resoled.
Soon I was attending movies and art shows. Finally
something happened that made me realize I was losing
my ability or desire to lead a normal work life. When I
wanted a change of pace from sitting in the office and it
wasn't near the middle of the day, I would tell my secretary that I would be visiting one or more branches to
study consumer patterns in those operations. This gave
me license to float around the city and suburbs for as
long as I wanted.

Alan, the Hustler

Managerial hustlers have been the subject of long-term
observation by psychologist Robert F. Pearse of Boston University's School of Management. In contrasting the managerial hustler to the sports hustler, he notes: "The managerial
hustler manipulates impressions by trying to make others
think he is *more* capable than he really is, and manipulates

situations in a way that will persuade others that he is *more* influential than he actually is. Whereas the sports hustler deliberately undersells his competence to bait his opponent, the managerial hustler oversells his competence to get others to reward and respect him beyond his desserts."[14]

Alan, an executive in the financial planning business, fits neatly into the subcategory of managerial hustler called the aggressive-articulate. According to Pearse, this type of hustler realizes early in life that in an impression-manipulating society, "being both aggressive and articulate gives him a strong chance of overwhelming less self-assured competitors. Coming on strong is his forte. He seldom bothers to acquire much technical expertise, leaving that to lesser mortals. Instead, he relies on his domineering manner and his ready flow of words. Even though he may not always understand his own words, his glibness, plus his air of conviction, tend to hard-sell those with whom he interacts into giving him what he wants."[15]

Alan's reliance on verbal polish and social sophistication as a substitute for technical competence led his company to the brink of bankruptcy. Alan had helped build a successful insurance agency that concentrated heavily on various forms of business coverage. Many of his agency's biggest accounts stemmed from social connections he had established with local politicians and businessmen. Alan received considerable help from his wife's socially prominent family in establishing insurance accounts. Two of his original accounts grew into corporate giants which gave his agency a substantial base of recurring business. Although Alan served as the initial contact person on many of the agency's major accounts, a few knowledgeable subordinates answered all the technical questions about insurance coverage.

Unilaterally, Alan decided that his agency should enter heavily into estate planning because the acquisition of new commercial business was beginning to decelerate. Despite admonitions from his subordinates that the uncertainty of the stock market made expansion into estate planning risky, Alan forged ahead. He insisted that his broad range of social contacts would attract some of the community's most influential citizens to the new program. "Estate planning is the way to go these days. Once we affiliate with Hamshire Capitol Corporation, we'll have hundreds of people converting the cash value of their life insurance policies into our exciting new *can't lose* proposition."

Ignoring the conservative (and technically sound) judgment of two of his subordinates, Alan arranged for expanded office space, elaborate promotional literature, and a series of posh public cocktail parties to introduce people to the new program of estate planning. Most of the funds for the new venture with Hamshire Capitol were taken from the agency's profits and reserves. A former subordinate describes what happened:

> Alan was correct in one respect. Hundreds of people did show up to see what we had to offer. We had an army of freeloaders coming to the bizarre spectacle of somebody promoting estate planning with alcohol and cocktail frankfurters. Many people ate, but very few bought. I think Dow Jones had a 40-point drop during the first three months of our affiliation with Hamshire Capitol. People liked Alan and wished him well, but his smoothness as a host couldn't bring us new business for a product that didn't fit the present economic cycle. Smooth talk couldn't make up for a bear market. Alan kept on telling the sales force that if they were more aggressive, most people would want to convert their old life insurance into our highly profitable plan. I don't think we generated enough new business in the first three months to pay for the cocktail parties and promotional literature.
>
> Alan finally saw the light and cut back on the estate-planning activities, but he wouldn't admit he was wrong. He kept mumbling some jargon about wanting to keep an eye open for diversification and maintain as many options as possible. I left because I could see that the agency was financially weakened by Alan's zealousness, combined with his poor technical knowledge. What Alan doesn't realize is that much of the success of

the agency was due to his wife's connections, dumb luck, and the common sense and insurance knowledge of a few people working for him. Alan is a phony who fools other people and himself. Sooner or later he'll get the agency into another deal that will destroy it.

Harriet, the Subcriminal Con Woman

Intelligent, enterprising Harriet is the president of Park City Realty Corporation. She learned many years ago that having good working relationships with real estate appraisers makes good business sense. Scattered observations convinced her that bank appraisers who knew her and liked her assigned her properties a slightly higher appraised value than those appraisers who did not know her personally. Realizing that good personal relationships are helpful in pushing borderline subjective judgments in her favor, Harriet decided to capitalize further on this business principle. She, as have been several hundred real estate investors who were indicted, decided to use personal influence to obtain favorable Federal Housing Authority property appraisals.[16]

Harriet's scandalous scheme followed the same pattern used by many other realtors involved in questionable dealings with the FHA. Step one involved locating a downtown, downtrodden single-family dwelling for a price of about $10,000. Most cities have more of these properties than the suburban homeowner would suspect. Step two was to make a variety of cosmetic repairs for about $2,500, performed by contractors who specialize in such repairs. (As one contractor working for Harriet noted: "I give anybody three prices on a roof repair. One to really do the job if you are going to keep the building. A lower price to take care of the building until you can sell it. And a third, to make your roof look good enough to keep the city inspectors off your back.")

Harriet would then locate a low-income buyer who could qualify for the very small down-payment FHA terms, anywhere from $200 to $500. Subcriminal behavior entered into the deal when Harriet suggested to an FHA appraiser: "Let's make a bet. I'll bet you one console model color TV set of your choosing that this solid little house in the city I just renovated will not receive an appraised value of its true worth, $17,500." After making an appraisal of $17,500, the FHA appraiser collects his or her TV set, but Harriet wins an even bigger prize. Obligingly, the FHA allows a $17,500 mortgage on the property, and Harriet realizes an immediate gross profit of about $5,000 on the property after making the cosmetic repairs.

A deviant act has been performed because the low-income homeowner (whom the FHA was trying to help) and the federal government got rooked. Once the owner discovers that the house needs extensive repairs that he cannot afford, he may abandon the property or discontinue making mortgage payments. As one deceived tenant explained, "I found out that all the piping in the ceiling was leaky. All the water stains had been covered up with paneling. When the leaks began to seep through, I was faced with a $750 repair bill. I couldn't pay both the plumber and the FHA, so I figured the bank could wait for their money." When tenants vacate the premises or stop making mortgage payments, the FHA is forced to take over the nearly unsaleable property.

Harriet and other members of her firm were involved in other deviant behavior with respect to low-cost housing that did not require "betting" with FHA officials. Recognizing that low-income buyers are often unsophisticated about spotting a dilapidated but cosmetically repaired property, Harriet sold several properties to low-income (including welfare) families. Few people at the lowest socioeconomic levels can afford to pay for major repairs. When they cannot afford to pay for needed repairs, the new owners abandon the property, then move in with relatives or rent an apartment. Harriet and her colleagues are considered deviant rather than shrewd or clever because they recognize that the purchasers of these properties will soon fall victim to the inadequacy of the cosmetic repairs. H. R. Crawford, an assistant secretary in the Department of Housing and Urban Development, observed: "It makes no sense to sell houses to welfare families. They don't have the means to take care of them."[17]

Don, the Pathological Liar

Don, a manufacturing manager in a large company, has a strong need to be well received by his boss, coworkers, and subordinates. He dislikes confrontation and feels acutely uncomfortable when h'e is cited as the cause of any management problem. Don's dislike of the consequences of being wrong or being the cause of harsh personnel actions leads him to construct an elaborate framework of distortions, half-truths and outright lies. People around him wonder why a person as creative and intelligent as Don incorporates so many lies into his management approach. From the standpoint of learning theory, one might say that so far in Don's life, lying about certain things brings him more pleasure than pain. Conversely, telling the truth about these same topics, he feels, would bring him more pain than pleasure. Don fabricates lies as he needs them, to fit a variety of business situations.

Don's company agreed to accept subcontracts on a private shipbuilding project. After weeks of careful negotiation, Don and his key subordinates agreed to have a set of custom-built pumps ready for shipment to the subcontractor by a tight, but not unrealistic, date. Thirty days before the promised delivery date, a representative of the prime contractor routinely inquired whether the pumps would be delivered on time. "I see absolutely no problem," replied Don. "My people tell me that we are about ready to ship and should have everything in your hands on or before the due date."

When the delivery date was missed and the prime contractor called, demanding an explanation, Don fabricated an excuse that probably would not be checked by the customer: "Oh, I thought you knew. We had a power generator failure in the plant that put us a little behind schedule on everything. By the time the turbine technicians put everything back in place, we found we were a month behind schedule. I anticipate no further delays."

Don constructs no less elaborate lies in dealing with his subordinates. Herb, his former manufacturing planning manager, reflects on Don's manipulation of information:

> Don is clearly the biggest liar I've met in corporate life. During our last performance review together, he told me he rated my performance as excellent and that he had recommended me for promotion to a manufacturing manager position in one of our biggest plants. That surely would have been a big position for me at this stage of my career. He told me that he would be back to me within about thirty days on the details. I was told that even if I didn't receive that promotion, I would be receiving a fifteen percent salary increase. I was so elated that I went around the company telling people what a pleasure it was to work for Don. I figured his reputation for telling half-truths was undeserved.
>
> Then things hit me like a bombshell. About a month later, Don called me into his office to tell me the company was undergoing a retrenchment and that my services would no longer be required. My successor, it turned out, was a friend of his from another company who was recently recruited into my department at Don's suggestion. When I tried to confront the liar about his plans to have me promoted to another plant, he told me business was no place to show emotion.

Don's boss, Reed, was also an unknowing recipient of his pathological lying. Reed and Don were having dinner together while on a business trip. Asked how things were going for him in the company, Don replied: "I'd say pretty damn good, Reed. Here I am at age 43, and I think I've finally found a corporate home. My plans are to both grow in my job and grow with this corporation. Loyalty, patriotism, and gratitude are sort of old-fashioned virtues, but these are things I really feel toward the company."

A week later, quite by accident, Reed discovered that Don

had registered with an executive search firm in hopes of finding a company presidency or a corporate executive job. Confronted by Reed about this peculiar discrepancy between their dinner conversation and this accidental bit of information about the executive search firm, Don replied: "Reed, for Gosh sakes, don't take that seriously. Somebody, quite unbeknownst to me, threw my name in the hat. You know these 'headhunters'; they will never reveal the source of the names they come up with for key positions."

Gordon, the Compulsive Gambler

Frank T., a member of Gamblers Anonymous—the compulsive gambler's equivalent organization to Alcoholics Anonymous—provides a dramatic description of a compulsive gambler: "A compulsive gambler goes in and loses all he has, pocket money, rent money, car payment money, kid's tuition money; then he goes out and steals some more, borrows from friends and family. One man I know ripped the rings off his mother's fingers, broke her arms and took the rings."[18]

Few compulsive gamblers in managerial positions exhibit such bizarre symptoms, but many allow gambling to interfere with their job effectiveness. Unlike some forms of managerial deviancy such as alcoholism and drug abuse, gambling does not leave telltale physical signs. Many of the problems created by compulsive gamblers in management ranks are similar to those created by stock market addicts. A good portion of their day is spent analyzing prospective investments and conferring with a broker or bookie. Gordon, now a member of a New York State chapter of Gamblers Anonymous, explains how gambling affected his career:

> I can tell you for sure that I am not currently gambling, even though I think I still have the disease. My current job title is systems analyst and that suits me just fine. It gives me a chance to be creative, to concentrate on something that makes a definite contribution to the company. When I tell friends that I'm working as a sys-

tems analyst, sometimes they kid me about knowing more about beating the system than anybody else. But the kidding doesn't bother me. I know I'm on the road back up again.

An important feature of this job is that it doesn't give me the freedom to place bets during the day. I share a cubicle with a young female systems analyst. It would be very embarrassing for me to pick up our extension phone to call a bookie to place a bet on the ponies or the Sunday football game. Being an analyst, I work under tight deadlines to get a given project accomplished, and it really helps. I was a manager of a management information group and it gave me too much freedom to make phone calls or visit gambling parlors during the day. I had a good team of people working for me who really didn't need much help from me on a day-by-day basis.

You want to know what specific effects my gambling had on my career? Being a gambling addict was worse than having two mistresses in addition to a wife and children. Of course, there were the money problems. When I was scoring well on my bets, finances were no problem. But when I was falling behind, I got pretty frantic. It was pretty hard to concentrate on a management problem like a budget review when I was on the brink of bankruptcy. I remember sitting in on one management meeting when I had a thousand dollars on a race that was being run at the very moment. Somebody nudged me and asked me if I was still with the group. I told them I had a toothache and had trouble concentrating.

Curiously, the home problems that stemmed from my gambling created more of an interference with my work than the actual gambling did. My wife would be on the phone with me at ten in the morning, pleading with me to stop gambling or to seek help. I remember once hitting our four-year-old son when he interrupted me while I was figuring out where I could raise some quick cash to get in a heavy poker game coming up that weekend. Realizing what I was doing to my family made it difficult for me to concentrate on my work for a week.

When I learned of some of the nicknames people in the company had developed for me, I knew my days were numbered. I was in the men's john one day, and I overheard two young programmers talking about me. Two names they used were "Gambling Gordie" and "Gordie the Greek." By the time I joined Gamblers Anonymous, my company and I had come to a mutual agreement about my leaving. The straight truth, though, is that I was fired.

Recent information gathered by *Dun's Review* indicates that businessmen make up a large proportion of compulsive gamblers in the United States because of their affluence and easy access to credit. Particularly significant is that "legalized gambling outlets such as offtrack betting and state lotteries do not seem to provide the excitement executives seek. According to Ralph F. Batch, director of the New Jersey Lottery, the average family income of the lottery ticket buyer is between $9,000 and $10,000, and nearly half are craftsmen, foremen, clerical or service employees."[19] Compulsive gamblers number anywhere from 5 to 10 million people in the United States. One can safely assume that at least 250,000 of these people are managerial workers.

The psychological roots of compulsive gambling, which are similar to any other personality disturbance, run deep. One might engage in psychological speculation about the typical motives of compulsive gamblers. Perhaps the generally accepted notion that the gambling addict has a strong need for self-punishment is accurate, but it is not particularly helpful from a management standpoint. Management intervention of any type can at best focus on the present and establish conditions that will help the managerial deviant overcome his or her deviancy.

Howard, the Abdicator

Howard is perhaps the most pernicious type of managerial deviant because he and others like him often go undetected for so long. In his hospital administrator's position, Howard's only real failing is that he is unable or unwilling to make a decision about all but the most trivial matters. Nicknamed "The Human Cipher" by his subordinates, Howard is admired by some for his cautiousness, restraint, and ability to look at problems from a "balanced point of view."

A clue to Howard's indecisiveness and capacity for inaction is revealed in his response to a vitriolic letter received from a patient complaining about inadequate hospital facilities. Three pages in length, the letter included charges that the water carafes were unclean and that the bed sheets were abrasive. Of greater significance, the irate patient inferred that she was investigating the possibility of filing a malpractice suit in relation to her spinal operation. Howard replied:

Dear Mrs. Jones:

Your letter to this hospital has been referred to my department. It has been read by me personally.
Sincerely,

Howard _____
Hospital Administrator

Another incident provides further understanding of Howard's reluctance to commit himself to a course of action. A newly formed firm in the community acted as a service bureau to hospitals and other organizations by taking complete charge of customer (in this case, patient) billing. When the company representative was referred to Howard, his response was: "I don't get paid enough to pass judgment on that kind of decision."

Howard's self-image was that of a modern manager. Here is how he described his management style in an interview: "I believe quite strongly in delegating responsibility to subordinates. There are few decisions that a boss must make. In a well-trained department every person is capable of making decisions that affect his own welfare. I try to lead, not push.

An effective manager is one who has a clean desk. A real manager should be thinking, not doing."

Does a technology, a systematic framework, a master plan, exist for dealing with Howard and the other managerial deviants described so far? I think it does. By combining the insights and practices of behavioral science—particularly behaviorism—and results-oriented management, it is possible to increase the probability that managerial deviancy can be brought under control without the wholesale dismissal of all managerial deviants. Behavioral science has provided a body of knowledge that can be and is being used to achieve many positive results in the control of aberrant behavior in management. An exposition of the nature of these techniques is the underlying purpose of this book.

2

Costs and Consequences

Managerial deviancy is not an isolated phenomenon involving only a handful of managers and staff people who create problems for their bosses, families, and themselves. Managerial deviants work within a larger system. As such, their errant behavior can have far-reaching consequences for their organization and society as a whole. One *value deviant* (a person whose personal values are deviant) who promotes people only on the basis of political favor can create a climate in his or her organization which provokes a talented executive to leave that organization in disgust. The executive who leaves the organization may contribute a breakthrough idea for the competition. A value deviant who discourages the employment of Puerto Ricans in his company—however well qualified they may be—might be contributing to the unfavorable economic conditions in the Puerto Rican section of town that lead to riot and insurrection. One paranoid middle manager who refuses to act on suggestions from a subordinate for fear of being shown up may have unwittingly shut out an idea that could have saved his company a million dollars.

Financial Costs

Alcoholism represents a good starting point in speculating about the costs of managerial deviancy, because it has been

27

the subject of more study and analysis than any other single form of deviancy in management. To begin, consider the total cost of alcoholism on the job, including both managerial and nonmanagerial personnel. According to information collected by the American Management Association in 1970, alcoholic workers cost their employers $8 billion annually.[1] The association states: "Eight-billion dollars is not an inflated figure. It may actually be a conservative estimate. . . ." Information gathered by *Time* in 1974 placed the dollar cost of alcoholism at a probable $15 billion a year, "much of it from lost work timé in business, industry and the Government." Although the area has been less intensively studied, there is no reason to believe that local, state, and federal government agencies have a lesser alcohol problem than do business and industry.

In assessing the costs of alcoholism among managerial workers, it is noteworthy that managers appear to be no more immune from alcoholism than nonmanagers. Anywhere from 4 to 8 percent of managers have drinking problems serious enough to classify them as alcoholics. As one caustic junior executive from an international corporation stated in a management development workshop: "If we fired all the alcoholics in our executive suite, our company would be left without managers. It's a status symbol to have a three-martini lunch." Considering that 10 percent of the work force is engaged in managerial work, the costs of alcoholism in management range from $800 million to $1.5 billion annually.

An easier way to visualize the cost of keeping an alcoholic manager on the payroll is to assume that he or she is costing the organization at least one-half of his or her salary plus benefits. The alcoholic is commonly referred to as the half-person. One well-integrated nonalcoholic normally does the work of two alcoholics of similar ability. Frequently the calibre of work performed by an alcoholic during dry periods is flawed. The temporary state of brain damage created by a bout of excessive drinking does not dissipate rapidly. In assessing the real costs of an untreated alcoholic, costs due to errors in judgment must also be estimated. A hotel

manager high on alcohol at the time decided to have the lob-
by walls painted fuchsia. When the job was completed, complaints from staff and guests necessitated a costly repainting.

Drug abusers in management tend to abuse themselves
with the "soft drugs" (marijuana, amphetamines) and not
hard drugs.[2] Thus the costs due to drug deviants in management concern mostly impaired judgment and some absenteeism, not outright criminal activities. Alcohol remains the
most dangerous drug used on a large-scale basis by managerial personnel. In situations where members of management
use expensive drugs (such as heroin, costing $50 to $100 per
day for the usual habit), two kinds of costly crimes can be
anticipated—thefts of goods and materials or the theft of
cash and checks.

Drug-related criminal behavior on the job by managers
and professionals is rare but not nonexistent. Stephen J.
Levy studied 95 drug abusers and addicts from New York
City, all on a voluntary basis. Job titles of this group included computer programmer, assistant factory manager, accountant, department store manager, dry cleaning store
manager, junior accountant, and purchasing agent.[3] Although the study did not relate specific crimes to specific individuals, it could easily be surmised that members of this
group were directly involved in stealing goods or money on
the job. One of those in the study, for example, forged an entire payroll.

In short, the aberrant behavior of virtually every managerial deviant has a cost. Overt forms of deviancy such as alcohol and drug addiction often have specific price tags.
More subtle forms of deviancy, such as managers who dis-
criminate against people on the basis of race, religion, or
sex, produce less tangible costs. A minority group coordinator in an industrial company presents this financial analysis:

> Top management has been moaning that our equal
> employment opportunity program is costing a bundle,
> much more than it is worth. I agree. I shouldn't be need-
> ed in this job and my function should not have been

created. If management had seen fit to treat black people equal to whites ten years ago, we wouldn't need a special program to give minority groups a fair shake. They brought this cost on themselves. But I can't blame the whole management team. One executive deserves the prize. He used to tell people how kind the company is to porters, to demonstrate that blacks were given a fair shake around here.

Bungling of Decision Making

Deviants in management bungle many, many decisions. Deviancy, in its multifarious varieties, clouds a person's judgment and leads to highly subjective, miscalculated decisions. Different forms of deviancy have different kinds of specific deleterious effects on decision making. In the long run, however, any form of deviancy can produce decisions that are dysfunctional to the organization.

Real Estate Developer. Mario, a value deviant, bungled a decision that has brought his company close to bankruptcy. As president of a real estate development corporation, Mario is obsessed with short-range profit. His stated business philosophy is "move in, make a quick profit, and get out. Nobody is in business for laughs." Mario's firm, Brent Developers, was responsible for the construction of a multimillion-dollar townhouse complex. Exquisite model townhouses—California redwood with ceiling-to-floor glass windows—were instrumental in achieving complete occupancy early in the development stages. Averaging $350-per-month rentals, this new development was admired by competitors and strongly demanded by prospective occupants. Tenants moved into the houses while much of the construction was still in progress. Amid rubble, rock-filled front yards, and muddy driveways, the tenants waited eagerly for outside (and some inside) construction to be completed.

Three months after moving in, each townhouse occupant received a notice that rentals were being increased 15 percent. According to the management, the original rent was the "construction rate." Now that construction was nearing completion, each tenant would be charged the full rent. Several tenants felt they had been duped and began to form a tenants' association. They didn't realize that this was only the first negative impact of Mario's deviant business philosophy.

As the firm headed toward financial trouble stemming from other unprofitable investments, Mario sought ways to raise quick cash for new investments, in order to compensate for his firm's other losses. His decision was to cancel the landscaping contract on the townhouses and cut back the maintenance crew to a skeleton staff. As calls for maintenance by the tenants went unanswered and the roads became muddier with the fall rains, tenants began to withhold rental payments. As the cash-flow problem was exacerbated, he cut back further on essential services. As subcontractors would no longer extend credit to Brent Developers, some minor internal work went uncompleted. With the company headed toward bankruptcy, it became impossible to attract new tenants to replace the many who were leaving. Mario's deviant decision to increase the cash flow by not following through on promised (and customary) land improvements and by unfairly hiking rents almost led to the demise of his company.

Community Relations Director.   Joanne, the director of community relations at a university, bungled several decisions relating to establishing a series of one-week seminars for professional and technical groups. Conducted by faculty members from different departments, these seminars required an average enrollment of about 25 participants to make a profit for the university. Usually, a large mailing succeeded by a follow-up ("Hurry up and enroll now") mailing is required to attract the proper number of participants to a given seminar. Brochures must be sent several months in advance (often because approval for attending the seminar must be secured).

Joanne made a bad decision about attending two consecutive seminars. She used too small a list in both instances, and she sent out the brochures only 45 days before the proposed seminar date. Underlying her poor decision making was her reliance on *downers*. She followed the infrequent practice of "shopping" for drugs—obtaining prescriptions for barbiturates from more than one physician (and placing her order at more than one pharmacy).

Joanne, agitated about her personal problems, used barbiturates to help her concentrate on her work. What she didn't realize was that barbiturates exerted a more negative impact on her work performance than did her agitation and restlessness.[4]

Blockage of New Ideas

A costly negative consequence of having pathologically indecisive people in managerial positions is that they prevent many potentially valuable ideas from surfacing. Managerial deviants of this type delay decision making about new ideas for two major reasons. First, they fear that accepting a new idea will imply that the old idea was either poor in the first place or that it has outlived its usefulness. The deviant of indecision fears being upstaged by an intelligent and enterprising subordinate. Second, accepting a new idea means that the manager will have to confront change, a potentially painful process. Should a subordinate's suggestions be valuable, they are likely to have far-reaching implications within the department or organization. Much of the managerial deviant's time will then be spent in making complicated readjustments and changes. For instance, assume that a subordinate suggests to a sales executive that the company should hire a sales force of their own rather than using manufacturer's representatives. If the sales executive agrees with this recommendation, the company must recruit and train an entire sales force—a complicated and time-consuming task.

Industrial Engineering Manager. A hidden danger in blocking a good idea from below is that the good idea will remain submerged only temporarily. Ideas suppressed in one organization by a managerial deviant often surface in a competitive organization. Chet, an industrial engineering manager, explains his experience in relation to having his best ideas blocked:

> My manager, Len, just wouldn't act on my plans and ideas. When I had something I thought was hot, he would tell me to put it in writing and he would give the matter careful consideration. When I followed up on the memo after putting it in writing, Len would talk about being overwhelmed with budgets, top executive meetings, etc. He would ask me to sit tight with my idea for awhile.
>
> The upshot was this. With the help of my small staff, I outlined a production and inventory control system that our plant sorely needed. I figured that this plan could be implemented for about $200,000 but that it would save us about $1.5 million per year. With the help of an outside consulting firm we could have this plan operational within ten months. Len just wouldn't move on my plan. He wouldn't say Yes or No; he just kept stalling. Finally I resigned and joined a company in a similar business. My new job title was Project Director, Production and Inventory Control System. Here was my chance to translate my ideas into action.

The Law of Delay. C. Northcote Parkinson has contributed considerable insights into the subject of the blockage of ideas in one of his less well-known works, *The Law of Delay*.[5] According to the law of delay, if you wish to kill an idea or project, you needn't reject it outright. Delay is a more effective form of denial. A procrastinator determines how much time is required to kill a proposal. If a supplier is on the verge of bankruptcy, a 30-day delay in paying a bill could destroy him. Herbert V. Prochnow, former president of the First National Bank of Chicago, explains how the law of delay often works:

> In government or business, the procrastinator seldom says, "Your idea is not good." With apparent helpfulness, he says, "We shall set up a committee to study it,

with subcommittees to deal with the various aspects of the idea." Then he emphasizes the need for research to discover all the facts. Fact finding becomes a substitute for thought. Memoranda begin to flow profusely in every direction. If 78 copies are needed, 100 are ordered because they cost little more. The extra copies go to the marginally interested. More and more persons at lower and lower levels spend longer and longer time reading what concerns them less and less. Finally, the idea is dead.[6]

Erosion of Morale

At a minimum, most forms of deviancy in management lower morale. Few people welcome working for a deviant, and some forms of deviancy are more insufferable than others. Lowered morale, in turn, can lead to other adverse consequences to the organization. Assuming that jobs are plentiful, people with low morale have a high propensity to quit. Unfortunately for the organization, it is the most capable people who have the best opportunity to join another organization. In some instances lowered morale can lead to decreased productivity. Morale is most closely related to productivity when an individual is not strongly self-motivated or when his or her work group has negative attitudes toward the company and its management.

The first awareness of the relationship between managerial deviancy and morale came to me incidentally to an attitude survey conducted in a manufacturing plant. A section of this survey gave people an opportunity to comment on any problem that was particularly vexing to them. Three production workers mentioned they were upset with the company because of an assistant foreman who "ran around the plant 'goosing' people."

An important factor underlying the depressing effect deviant behavior has on morale is that nondeviant people object to what they perceive as a double standard. Management is frequently lax in the performance standards set for deviants

of many varieties, while the nondeviant person is held to
high performance standards. Kemper Insurance has carefully documented the kinds of behavior exhibited by an on-the-
job alcoholic. When such deviation from expected business
decorum is manifested by a member of management, the
morale of subordinates and coworkers is subject to depression. Following is a list of the behavioral problems observed
in the alcoholic during the stage of alcoholism where drinking is unmistakably related to work-performance problems:

Avoids boss and associates, or becomes grandiose or
belligerent.

Swings in work pace become more pronounced and
more frequent.

Overall performance quite unsatisfactory. Many work
problems that had previously been partially hidden or
ignored may come to supervisor's attention.

Changes in excuse patterns. Excuses even more elaborate and sometimes bizarre.

More frequent and more severe hangovers on the job.

Attendance becomes unreliable.

Severe financial difficulties.

More frequent and more severe off-the-job accidents.

Frequent use of breath purifiers to cover morning drinking during working hours.

Changing work patterns to assure sneaking drinks during the day.

Increased nervousness, gastric upsets, and insomnia
problems.

Occasional complaints from customers of the company.

Marked increase, in some instances, of hospital-medical surgical claims.[7]

Exodus of Competent People

The deviant behavior of management frequently drives competent people out of an organization. Deviancy fosters lowered morale, and lowered morale can lead to turnover, providing the dissatisfied individual has the wherewithal to find another suitable position. Competent people are usually those with the formal credentials and informal characteristics necessary for mobility.

Brokerage Firm Manager.   Dick, a former stockbroker, describes how his former manager, an ethical deviant, encouraged turnover in his branch of a prestigious, nationwide brokerage house:

> We called this character, "Crazy Mike." He was a six-foot-five, redheaded Irishman who was the most task-oriented son of a bitch anybody ever worked for. All of the sales reps in his department were treated as if they were convicts trying to break out of prison. Mike's approach to supervising us was particularly bad because we were in the beginning of a bear market and people were becoming skittish about investing heavily in the market. Mike had an approach to motivation nobody who worked for him could ever forget. Here is a good example of what I'm talking about. Let's say our firm was handling a new offering for some marginal stock like "Columbian Utilities." Mike would announce something like, "Okay, every bastard in this department is going to unload his quota of Columbian. I don't care who you call or what you tell them, just unload this issue. Call your grandmother, your uncle, your best man. I don't give a good goddamn. Just move that stuff out the door."

Mike's pep talk was just the beginning. He would pace up and down the aisles at an increasing rate as the day went by. The lower the sales, the faster he would pace. His words of inspiration went something like this, "Nobody here is going to leave his desk until you've sold your share of Columbian. No coffee breaks, no trips to the water cooler, twenty minutes for lunch, and five minutes for the can. I don't care if your head is buzzing inside from making phone calls. If you want your job, get your sales pinned down. Forget that crap about professionalism. You're a bunch of peddlers and don't you forget it for one minute."

Crazy Mike drove a large number of good people out of the brokerage business. Rather than look for a job with a competitor, many of us just left the securities business. I suspect Mike will have a heart attack and retire early, but in the meantime he's doing a lot of damage.

Avoidance of Political Career. As with other types of deviants, ethical deviants drive good people out of organizations. They also exert a negative force of equal or greater significance. Deviants tend to dilute the source of supply of new blood into the organization. For example, the occupation of *politician* dwindled in prestige among high school and college students during the last two years of the Nixon administration. College students often talked derisively about a career in public service because of the large-scale exposure of ethical and moral deviance by the President of the United States and many of his staff advisors. As an MBA (Master of Business Administration) student told his classmates in a formal discussion of career choices:

Four years ago I was idealistic; I wanted to become a public servant and help humanity. Now, I'm convinced that I can best serve humanity by doing something honest like running a small business. My thinking has been completely turned around. A racetrack owner is a saint in comparison to many politicians I've read about.

When the Vice-President [of the United States] is a thief
who cavorts with other criminals, the field of politics is
in deep trouble. I'd rather tell my folks I was opening a
bookie operation than say I was going to Washington."

Misallocation of Resources

Systems Manager. Tom enjoys sex and alcohol—two
normal desires in most cultures. This system manager's behavior is deviant and costly to his employer only because he
indulges in sex and alcohol on company time. A reasonable
proportion of his salary and benefits is misallocated. Company funds are expended for a full-time systems manager,
yet Tom is preoccupied with noncompany matters about 15
percent of a normal workweek. Tom's noonday diversions
are costing the company a minimum of $4,500 per year since
his salary and benefits package is approximately $30,000 a
year, and this is a conservative estimate. Tom's assistant
cannot devote full time to his job. Some must be diverted to
cover for Tom during his absences. Time spent performing
Tom's work could probably be more profitably invested in
something constructive, like developing a new system for
the company.

Chief Engineer. Pathological lying is another form of
deviancy that results in the misallocation of resources. A
pathological liar will often tell costly lies to management in
order to protect his or her power and self-esteem. Larry, the
chief engineer in an industrial company, recognized that the
low-friction gear his department was developing had little
probability of becoming marketable and profitable. But,
lacking a good alternative product to develop, he insisted
that management continue to invest money and human resources in the gear. Two years later it became apparent to
others that the new product was a failure. Unquestionably
the money and manhours invested in the gear could have
been allocated to an alternative use—some product with a
higher probability of achieving an adequate return on investment. Lying can be costly.

CREEP. A familiar economic fact of life is that business

organizations face complex, competing demands for their capital. When money is invested in quasi-legal or illegal pursuits, it is reasonable to conclude that resources have been misallocated. Many stockholders, for example, would prefer that money be invested in new-product development or social projects than in questionable campaign contributions. CREEP (the Committee for the Reelection of the President), operating before the 1972 presidential election, developed some elaborate schemes for pressuring companies to make illegal campaign contributions. Had stockholders been informed of these matters, many would have chosen a more ethical allocation of resources. The how of these morally deviant practices is explained by *Newsweek*:

> A corporation can resort to a variety of dodges. American Airlines, for instance, had a Lebanese broker send it a phony bill. American's accountants didn't know the $55,000 it paid to cover the bill actually wound up with CREEP.
>
> The use of a bogus invoice is perhaps the most popular ploy. . . . Ashland Oil, whose books are audited by Ernst & Ernst, drew $100,000 from a subsidiary in Gabon. The money was "laundered" by passing it through a Swiss bank. Finally, it was delivered to the Nixon campaign. American Ship Building Co. is charged with awarding phony "bonuses" to eight trustworthy corporate officials—together with a list of GOP committees to give the money to.
>
> "There are a hundred ways this can pass by an auditor," says Phillip Moore of the Washington-based Project on Corporate Responsibility. "I'm sure that there are thousands of corporate campaign contributions that will never be known."[8]

Waste of Human Resources

Perhaps the most crucial reason why a system is needed for combating managerial deviance is that deviant behavior in management frequently results in a waste of human resources. Deviance can result in denied or truncated opportunities for large numbers of people. Managerial deviants are often found in "gatekeeper" positions where they have the power to prevent people from entering positions with good potential for high income and recognition. Other forms of deviance can result in physical harm or possibly injury and death to people.

Sexism. Job discrimination against women is a form of moral deviance, particularly when it is practiced in spite of considerable federal legislation outlawing such discrimination. Discriminating against women is a waste of human resources simply because many women who *might have been effective in higher-level jobs* are denied the opportunity of making such a contribution. Societal forces such as early conditioning by parents and teachers must share the blame for job discrimination against women, but a large number of moral deviants in key positions have served as an influential factor in preventing women from moving into the executive suite. A key manufacturing executive (male) told me bluntly: "Of course I would never agree to having a woman executive in our company. No matter how brilliant she was about business, she would probably be a bitch to work for. Women make very unreasonable bosses."

Hard data gathered by *Fortune* magazine documents how women have been systematically excluded from true executive positions in American industry. In the process of identifying the 10 highest-ranking female executives in big business, *Fortune* researchers dug up some dramatic figures about sexism at the top of organization.[9] (Rigorous standards were set for a *key executive.*) Few women make it through to the top of big business. Men outnumber women by 600 to 1 in elite executive positions in the 1,300 largest companies in the United States.

The Security and Exchange Commission reports on each company studied. Among the information called for in these reports are the names and salaries of the three highest-paid officers of the company, "provided they earned more than $30,000 each, and to report any director earning over $30,000." The names of only eleven women showed up among some 6,500 officers and directors. These figures cannot be explained away by the fact that there are no women to choose from. According to the 1973 Economic Report of the President, about 3 percent of all women in the work force fell into the category of "managers and administrators." Thus if sexism were not an influential factor, we could expect something near 200 female executives among the 6,500 key posts in question.

Racism. Job discrimination against black males, which prevents blacks with management potential from gaining entrance into managerial jobs, is a similar waste of human resources. An overall trend exists for decreasing discrimination against black males in management, but blacks are still underrepresented in key jobs.[10] Twelve percent of whites in the work force were classified as "Proprietors, Managers, and Officials" in 1960 and 1970, and this figure will probably hold true for 1980. Correspondingly, the percentage of black workers classified as "Proprietors, Managers, and Officials" for 1960 and 1970 is 2.3 and 3.5. A reasonable extrapolation is that by 1980 about 7 percent of the black work force will occupy such positions.

Despite these impressive statistical gains for blacks in management, many black people included in these statistics are prevented from exercising leadership. A black manager in a commercial bank explains how this subtle form of discrimination works:

> Many of these manager titles held by blacks are pseudomanagement jobs. The worn-out joke about being the "token black" is still a valid observation. A lot of black people in the bank industry are called managers, yet they have no subordinates reporting to them. I would regard it as an insult to be called a manager yet given no real management responsibility.
>
> A college friend of mine was the classic example of the "show black." Jim was the ideal type for industry. Handsome and personable, he was also the captain of the football team. Thus we could assume he had talent for leading people. A San Francisco bank put him in

their management training program. Three years later
he was given a manager's title and put out front on the
platform where people could see his gorgeous black
face. But the trouble was, the only thing he supervised
was his in-basket.

Child Labor Abuse.   Moral deviancy in management also
takes its toll on the physical well-being of some children
and adolescents, particularly in the agricultural industry.
Child labor on the farm remains a national scandal. *Time*
notes that hundreds of thousands of children are working in
fields all around the country. "They labor in the cherry orchards of Michigan, the peach orchards of Colorado, the tomato fields of New Jersey, the bean fields of Oregon. The
practice is especially flagrant in California, the richest
agricultural state."[11] Only about 20 percent of migrant farm
children remain in school beyond the sixth grade. Even
when they are formally attending school, many of them are
more likely to be found in the field than in the classroom
during the fall harvesting season.

In addition to rewarding families for keeping their children in the fields and out of school, farm management that
makes extensive use of child labor is controlling costs at the
expense of children's health. Lendon Smith, a pediatrician
from Portland, Oregon, has observed that crouching, bend-
ing, or staying in one position for long periods of time in the
fields can arrest the normal physical development of
children.[12]

A word of caution is in order. Not all harvesting by children reflects deviant behavior by farm management. Sometimes the school system allows for this practice. In Maine
during the potato picking season school begins a month early so the children will be out of school in time to help with
the harvesting.

Death.   Alcoholism, it can be safely argued, is the form of
managerial deviancy with the greatest effect on human resources. About half of each year's 55,000 deaths in automobile accidents involve drivers or pedestrians under the influence of alcohol. Several hundred of these deaths can be

traced directly to the alcoholic behavior of managerial personnel. A positive program of rehabilitating alcoholics in management might have prevented as many as half of these deaths. Managers sometimes kill each other in alcoholism-related accidents. The following bizarre accident happened in upstate New York, as described by a researcher in managerial deviance:

> Four of the company executives drove up to Syracuse to attend a banquet for the chairman who was retiring after 40 years service with the company. After the banquet the party of four had a few more rounds of drinks at a topless bar. Instead of staying at the hotel overnight, they decided to drive back home. The trip was about fifty miles. If they hadn't been drinking so heavily, they would never have headed back on a five-degree-below-zero night.
>
> About 40 minutes after they left, Delbert, our manufacturing head, told the driver to stop the car so he could relieve himself. The other three were so drunk that they drove off and left Delbert out in the snow on one of the coldest nights of the winter. Although a truckdriver picked him up on the side of the road, half-frozen, he never recovered. Delbert died in a hospital a week later from pneumonia and overexposure. Now the company verbally reprimands anybody known to drink heavily at company functions.

Long-Range Adverse Consequences

Value and ethical deviancy in top management often have long-term adverse consequences to the organization, which are not immediately apparent to people interested in maximum profits. A question many executives now ask themselves and each other is "What is the negative impact to the organization of not taking a socially responsible view?" An ethically deviant point of view may prove to have a few isolated short-range advantages, but they may be dysfunctional

in the long run. Referring again to the child farm-labor issue, fruit growers who do not soon find an alternative to
child labor may be forced out of business in several years by
formal legislation. Unmechanized and unable to pay *adult
wages,* fruit growers may find it uneconomic to continue
operation.

Henry Ford II showed some awareness of the long-range
adverse consequences of moral deviancy in management
when he explained to the stockholders of Ford Motor Company that his determined effort to recruit workers from De-
troit's hard-core unemployed was a preventive measure
against the resurgence of ghetto riots, which would threaten
the company.

Albert Z. Carr, in his compelling article, "Can an Executive Afford a Conscience?", reports that "when a number of
life insurance companies agreed to invest in slum recon-
struction at interest rates somewhat below the market, their
executives were quick to forestall possible complaints from
the stockholders by pointing out that they were opening up
new markets for life insurance."[13] The ethically deviant approach would have been for these companies to contend that
"business is business; why give preferred rates to people
with poor ability to repay loans?"

The positive long-range consequences of not being morally deviant were underscored in a *Fortune* survey of chief executives of the largest corporations in the United States. Ten
percent of these executives maintained a philosophy of
profit maximization. Nearly all of this 10 percent, however,
reported that their firms were directly involved in social programs such as training hard-core unemployed persons. Executives in this study "saw profit and public service connected through a complex pluralistic social system. By engaging in public service they were able to maintain an environment favorable to their profitable operation."[14]

Contagion of Deviancy

An unfortunate consequence of managerial deviancy is
that it is contagious. Deviancy from above spreads perni-

ciously throughout the organization. A top management team that discriminates against women or blacks, that keeps an alcoholic chairman of the board on full salary and privileges, or that uses the company plane to fly friends around the country is contributing to a climate of deviancy. As one aggravated young salesman complained: "Why should I be back in the office on Friday afternoon at 4:30, filling out call reports, while my boss and his boss are out playing golf?"

A plant manager was being pressured for an explanation of why he had not achieved his quota of providing employment opportunities for women and minority groups in his plant. His response was:

> I want to do my share of giving everybody an equal chance, but that quota system is just another chore for me and my staff. Besides, the whole idea of hiring more women and blacks is just a public relations gimmick by our president. Somebody in public relations writes an elegant speech for the president. He delivers the message to the newspapers and then expects us to implement his grand schemes.
>
> Two years ago our president was hot on hiring the handicapped. Now he's hot on hiring more minorities and women for key jobs. But his whole approach is wrong. He sets a very poor example. Look around the executive offices. Nobody around there, not even a clerk, is physically handicapped. The only black around the executive office works as a maintenance man. The best job any woman has up there is executive secretary. If our president really wanted to do some social good, he could set a positive example for the rest of the organization. When the president really doesn't care about social problems, I doubt he cares if the people who really operate this company have a social conscience.

3

Predisposition to Deviance

Managerial deviancy may be traceable to factors primarily within the individual, those primarily outside of the individual, or a combination of internal and external factors. Wayne, a warehouse manager who fills his automobile gasoline tank from a company pump, may be manifesting this deviant behavior for various reasons. He may have a long-standing personality quirk that allows him to pilfer on a minor scale without qualm. He may be working in a job environment that unofficially condones such action as standard business practice; free gasoline, within limits, is considered an informal part of management compensation at his company. Or he may have a tendency toward dishonesty, which will surface only when a good opportunity presents itself—*situational ethics.*

Inadequate Response to Pressure

A vital characteristic for a manager to possess is the capacity to work effectively under pressure. The person who "chokes" under the amount and type of stress considered average by others is ill suited for significant managerial responsibility. Nevertheless, some people work their way into high-level management positions without having the necessary mechanisms for coping with heavy job pressures. Among the many inadequate responses to stress are various forms of deviancy.

Marketing Executive. John, the former director of marketing in an aerospace company, exhibited the deviant behavior of *extreme withdrawal* in response to the job pressure of declining business. His major responsibility was providing overall direction to the marketing effort of the aerospace division of a large electronics company. In his midthirties, John was experienced in his work and was considered to have potential for higher-level executive work. His subordinates and his boss regarded him as a quiet and slightly introverted but competent administrator. His general approach to business problems was a combination of management by objectives and management by exception. After he and his subordinates agreed on overall objectives for the quarter, he asked to be consulted only about significant problems in reaching business objectives ("pressing" problems).

A series of business problems did manifest themselves, and they exerted more pressure than John could tolerate. Accustomed to the volatile nature of the aerospace industry, John regarded some fluctuations in business as routine. The year 1971, however, was an extraordinary departure from routine. By the third quarter, 12 months had passed without his division of the company receiving a new contract. As the backlog of orders diminished, the sales managers reporting to John became increasingly concerned. Despite an intensified effort to find new business, no orders were forthcoming.

John's deviant behavior pattern in response to the stress of no new business was to withdraw from his subordinates. At first, he was merely difficult to contact. His secretary was instructed to parry telephone calls from everybody but customers or his immediate superior, the vice-president of marketing. As the telephone calls increased, John's secretary was given new instructions. She delayed callers by telling them: "John is in serious negotiations today and cannot be disturbed. Can I be of assistance?" Several of his subordinates attempted to reach him at home. Members of his family were told to tell them that he was "out of town on emergency business."

Next, John began to withdraw from his colleagues and boss. Frustrated by John's aloofness, his boss sent him a lengthy memo, describing plans for a company-wide retrenchment and reduction in force to adjust for declining business. Three days later the memo was returned to his boss with the cryptic statement: "Your plans have been carefully reviewed. I will provide you an action plan as soon as humanly possible considering the exigencies of the situation." As his deviant behavior became more blatant, John was finally assigned to a product-planning position in another division of the company.

Chamber of Commerce Executive. Bill, an executive in a city Chamber of Commerce, is a controlled alcoholic. He usually confines his drinking to nonworking hours and almost never appears at the Chamber adversely influenced by alcohol. At business luncheons he orders tomato juice in place of a cocktail. His manifestation of aberrant behavior occurred in a probably never-to-be-repeated situation that caused him considerable embarrassment but not his job. One day late in May, Bill received an unexpected call from the principal of a high school about fifty miles away. The principal asked Bill to substitute as the June commencement speaker because of the sudden cancellation of a scheduled speaker. Reluctantly he accepted, recognizing that such an assignment was fraught with stress.

As graduation day approached, Bill became increasingly agitated and began to drink more than usual at night. Despite his increased drinking, he prepared a commencement address entitled, "America: Opportunities and Challenges." Bill's tension level rose to new heights on graduation day. In an attempt to calm himself, he arrived in the town where the school was two hours early. The high school principal describes what happened:

> Bill set a very poor example for the Chamber of Commerce. He was the only speaker in the history of Coolidge High School to fail to make it to the ceremonies. I

guess the fellow just got shook about giving his speech. He apparently went over to the hotel in the afternoon and decided to loosen up with a drink. He sure loosened up. Just before the ceremonies, somebody finally found him lying in a gutter in a semistupor. He was in no shape to go on stage. I covered for him by giving a three-minute greeting and well wishes talk. I can only imagine how humiliated poor Bill must have felt.

Compensation for Inadequacies

Recividists frequently lament that they return to crime or other forms of asocial behavior because the straight (non-criminal) world will not provide them an opportunity to earn a legitimate living. Similarly, some situations of managerial deviance can be attributed to managers and entrepreneurs who resort to deviant behavior because they are not equipped to earn a high income through legitimate means. One such compensation for inadequacies is perhaps illustrated by the alleged fraud involved in the promotion of a memorial album for the late Pittsburgh Pirate outfielder, Roberto Clemente. The promoter was indicted for allegedly retaining $185,000 of the proceeds for himself.[1] The prosecutor said that proceeds from the sale of the record album were supposed to be used to establish a "youth city" in Puerto Rico to aid culturally disadvantaged boys. According to charges made in the indictment, no money was ever turned over to the Clemente Fund or any other group in Puerto Rico.

Sexual exploitation of subordinates is a clear example of a manager resorting to deviant behavior to compensate for felt inadequacies. A manager who was able to establish satisfactory sexual relationships, using his personal appeal, would not have to resort to abuse of power. Clyde, the insurance executive described in Chapter 1, used the company career acceleration program as a vehicle for having affairs with young women. Had he felt adequate enough to find women on his own, he would not have found it necessary to use promises of promotion as inducements for sex. As with most forms of managerial deviancy, Clyde's behavior was self-defeating. His approach to improving his social life through the abuse of power led to the termination of his employment with the company.

Stress in Personal Life

Reactions to personal crises are multiform. Healthy, well-integrated individuals are able to cope with personal setbacks even if they succumb to such traumata for a short period of time. Many executives—male and female—have displayed temporary bouts of deviancy of one form or another under the pressures of a family death or wayward romance. Deviancy in any form, from drug abuse to absenteeism, can stem from a person's inability to constructively handle substantial personal setbacks or disappointments. Unfortunately, deviancy as a response to stress leads to more rather than less stress. Deviant behavior exhibited in the work environment leads to pressures that make it more difficult to handle problems at home. Intensified problems at home, in turn, make it more difficult to properly manage problems at work.

The spiraling effect of deviancy as a response to stress can be illustrated by the situation of a manager who gambles at horse racing to escape from job pressures. As job pressures mount, he increases the time and money invested in horse racing. Assuming that his losing far exceeds his winning, he will probably encounter disapproval from family members. Arguments over other matters multiply because of the problems created by excessive gambling. Frequent arguments at home further lessen the manager's ability to concentrate at work. He performs even more poorly in response to job pressures because of lowered concentration. His gambling activity is further increased because of his now intensified need to escape from job pressures (and recoup some of his financial losses).

A deviant response to family problems is exemplified by a data processing manager who was on the verge of being fired by his company because of a series of unexplained absences. During a luncheon conference he offered his boss this straightforward rationale for his behavior: "How the hell do you think you would react if you found out your wife was having an affair with your minister? I just can't bring myself to concentrate on my job."

Manufacturing Vice-President. Psychiatrist Jerome Steiner reports a case history that further illustrates the reciprocal relationship between work and family problems—but in this situation work problems precipitated personal problems.

At age 45, Frank Brown is a self-made man. Although he has no academic degrees or special training, Brown was recently promoted to the vice presidency of a medium sized manufacturing company. He is known as an assertive man who makes friends easily and is very active in community affairs. He is married, has a son who was recently married and a daughter in college.

Despite many physical complaints, Brown is in good condition, other than being slightly overweight. His complaints include "gall bladder attacks (no physiological basis found for these), "allergic" irritation of the eyes, lower back pain, and insomnia. He was referred to a psychiatrist after his intestinal discomforts were unrelieved by medical treatment.

After being discharged from the Army, Brown obtained a supervisory position in a large West Coast city. He married soon after and was sent to a branch office in the Midwest. He worked his way through staff positions and was eventually asked to set up an office in another city.

The family relocated and their first child was born. After spending five years in the new city, Brown accepted a more lucrative job, and the family moved again. He remained in this position for several years, having little difficulty in organizing and running a small office while he and his wife became involved in community activities and extensive entertaining. A second child was born.

Brown then accepted a job organizing an office for a new company, and his business responsibilities increased to include the hiring of staff and the supervision of middle-management personnel. He had little contact with lower echelon personnel in the organization thereafter, but was well liked by the "management team." It was during this period that Mrs. Brown developed a number of psychosomatic complaints and the children began to manifest behavioral disorders necessitating referral to a child-guidance clinic.

The growth of the corporation resulted in management moving to another city. Mrs. Brown resented this move, but accepted it. After several years Brown began to feel that his outside activities were somehow not pleasing; he no longer looked forward to lodge and church meetings. His wife became active in various organizations, but the couple had few activities in common other than those involving Brown's business associates.

As his responsibility grew, Brown found that he had to spend increasing amounts of time "checking" his subordinates and ensuring the smooth operation of his branch of the organization. His social life began to be restricted to business contacts, and even his occasional golf games were with people he knew in the business world. He became briefly depressed, but he was not aware of feeling this emotion predominantly.

Mrs. Brown suffered a more severe depression, consulted several psychiatrists, and began to take tranquillizing and antidepressant medication. The couple's sexual life dwindled and eventually stopped. It was during this time that Brown was referred to the psychiatrist. In addition to his physical problems, he complained that his wife did not understand him and had little sympathy for his discomfort. He also felt that he could no longer communicate with his children.

Now, at times of business expansion and business activity, Brown's depression is relieved and he is unaware of any difficulties. His physical complaints remain, however, and his secretary has taken the role of "nurse." The marital adjustment of his son has not been good, his daughter has been involved in numerous antisocial and rebellious activities, and his wife has become a regular psychiatric patient.[2]

Noteworthy in the case history of Brown is that although he began to show signs of ineffectiveness in his management style, his behavior fell short of deviancy. Intervention by the psychiatrist may have been an influential factor in preventing a worsening of the adverse effect Brown's problems at home were having on his work behavior. His problems at home appeared to have been precipitated by his wife's adverse reaction to his frequent relocation.

Mid-Life Crisis

Few people entering large, complex organizations achieve their goals of holding executive rank. Most lose out in the competition for top jobs. At approximately age 40, those who recognize that they are confined to the purgatory (in their perception) of a career in middle management gradually develop a morose attitude. It dawns on them that the high aspirations they established at the beginning of their careers will not be attained. Psychologist Harry Levinson uses age 35 as the entry point into middle age.[3] By this time in life, most career people have enough data to make a realistic assessment of their success and failure pattern in life. Information gathered by Lee Stockford of the California Institute of Technology indicates that about five out of six men in professional and managerial positions undergo a period of frustration in their middle thirties.[4] According to Stockford's survey, one person in six never fully recovers from this mid-life crisis.

Product Manager. Among the aberrant responses to the crisis of middle age are alcoholism and drug abuse. Levinson notes that the peak in executive alcoholism is in the 35–55 age bracket. A more complex form of managerial devi-

ance was exhibited by David, a product manager, in response to his frustrated ambitions. A former colleague described David's aberrant behavior:

People who knew David gradually realized he was
going out of his tree. It all seemed to begin with his being passed over for a director position. He always talked
the company game and acted as if he were the candidate
in line for the marketing vice-president. David went on
a two-week vacation after the announcement that somebody else was getting the job he wanted. To everyone's
surprise, he returned a changed man.

First of all, his clothing was completely changed. He
had dressed in a conservative, businesslike manner before. Now he was the guy with the supermod clothing.
It looked as if he may have bought a hairpiece. A few of
us began to notice that David was beginning to drink
heavily, but he was not outright drunk at work. He
saved his heavy drinking for parties. Once we had an
after-five cocktail party to celebrate the introduction of
a new product. Two of us had to carry David out the
building and take him home.

I knew David was slipping, more because of his an-
tics around the office than his drinking and change in
clothing style. He became a dreadful time-waster of
both his own time and that of other people. He was forever urging somebody to "escape this madness for a few
minutes and have a cup of coffee." A few people in the
department would close their door when David approached. They did this because he interpreted an open
door as an invitation to enter your office and sit on your
desk for 20 minutes, chatting about nothing directly related to work. A friend of mine and I developed a signal
to use in getting David out of either of our offices. If
David was sitting on my desk or in the chair in my
office, and my friend walked by, I would put my right
hand on my head if I wanted David out of the office. My
friend would then buzz me on the intercom system, and
I could legitimately say, "Excuse me, this is a call I've

been expecting." David finally left the company when
he inherited some money. He bought a small fishing
tackle store in Maine which I hear is doing poorly.

People in fields other than business also face the mid-life
crisis. William J. Constandse, a businessman, makes a per-
ceptive observation about college professors:

> . . . after the first hurdle of tenure has been successful-
> ly cleared, the going gets rough. He faces stiff competi-
> tion from other professors who always seem to be able
> to get research grants, find enough time and inspiration
> to publish scholarly . . . papers, and know the right
> people so that they are invited to address scientific
> seminars and meetings. And so they, too, join the silent
> majority of disillusioned individuals over forty years of
> age.[5]

Faulty Self-Structure

People in key jobs sometimes become deviant simply because they have not developed personal values with which
to guide their day-to-day behavior. However amorphorous
this concept sounds, it can be an important determinant of
behavior. The self-structure is "the center of the individual's world of experience and his reference point for evaluat-
ing and coping with his environment."[6] Once the self-structure begins to develop, the individual tends to maintain it
and behave in ways consistent with that structure.

Developing a strong self-structure, according to Coleman,
requires that a person find reasonably accurate answers to
three questions: (1) Who am I? (2) Where am I going? and
(3) Why?[7]

Executive Search Consultant. Phil, an executive search
consultant, had more trouble answering these questions
than do most people, a factor that could have been contributed to his form of managerial deviancy.

Phil was a history major in college, taught high school his-

tory and political science for awhile, and then joined a large
company as a management trainee. After 10 years of a medi-
ocre career in lower middle management, Phil got a position
as an executive search placement counselor. His motivation
for joining was clear-cut: "It sounded like a fun way of turning over a few bucks. Nothing else I had done for a living
seemed very profitable or gave me any kicks." Phil describes
his form of deviant professional behavior without any visible signs of guilt. Asked about his cleverest technique, Phil
commented:

> We call this one the "comparison technique." Let's
> say a client of ours requests that we find them a new
> manufacturing head at 40 G. That means an $8,000 fee
> for us if we can turn up a candidate that fits their needs.
> Manufacturing people on the loose who can really do
> the job are tough to find. We can certainly locate a
> bunch of lower-level people with average experience
> who would definitely not fit the specifications laid
> down by the client. So we have to keep on digging.
> Let's assume that we only turn up one manager who
> in our opinion could really do the job for the client, at
> least in a passable manner. Once we are convinced, then
> we have to convince the company that hired us that this
> guy is their man. Quite often that's tough. The client
> figures he's paying a load of money to the candidate and
> to us, so he should be given the chance to see some top-
> notch candidates. We figure that the client has to take
> the one candidate we've turned up because there are
> very few manufacturing heads looking for work. Here is
> where the comparison technique fits.
> We tell the client we have two pretty good candidates
> for their inspection. The first candidate we send over is
> really marginal, at least the way he comes across to peo-
> ple. It's no problem sending the client a marginal candi-
> date to look at. There are always a load of marginal peo-
> ple looking for a new position. A couple of days later,
> we send the candidate we really want to sell to the cli-
> ent. Quite often the client will be highly impressed with

the second candidate because he looks so good in comparison to the first candidate we referred to them.

Self-Defeating Tendencies

Entrepreneur.   Mr. Adams was sent by his family doctor to the psychologist and psychoanalyst, Benjamin B. Wolman. Adams' wife told Wolman that her husband was heading toward physical, mental, and financial catastrophe. Wolman describes the case, based on his therapy notes:

> Mr. Adams was a mild-mannered, polite man. He was the only child of poor parents. He had worked hard, and about 25 years ago had started his own business, assisted by two friends. Mr. Adams was a man of unusual financial abilities; one of his two friends was a production wizard, and the other a sales genius. After many years of struggle, Mr. Adams and his associates had developed a major business enterprise.
>
> For awhile, everything went well: the business grew and expanded. They built a new plant and acquired modern machinery; their products were selling well. Two years ago Mr. Adams' two associates had asked for modest increases in their piece of the business. This would have cost Mr. Adams little, if anything, considering taxes. The logical thing would have been to do it. But Mr. Adams reacted irrationally. He berated his two friends and flatly refused to give them a dime more—even though the marketing head warned that he would go to work for a competitor, and he would take with him half of the customers.
>
> The partners left and Adams was in difficulty. At this same time he started a lawsuit against an architect who was supervising the construction of a house for him. Mr. Adams began to quibble with foremen, bookkeepers, and secretaries. He was at odds with whoever worked for him.

At home as well, Mr. Adams was irritable and quarreled with his wife and children. He could not sleep at night because consciously he was struggling to *save* the company while unconsciously he was doing everything to destroy it.

Did he know what he was doing when he fought with his partners? Undoubtedly he did. He said to me: "When this guy came and asked me for a little more money, I told him that he was not my friend . . . knowing damn well that, if I were in his position, I would do exactly what he did—and be justified in doing it. Why do I do these things to myself? I just can't help it."[8]

Adams' form of managerial deviancy stemmed from self-defeating behavior that is characteristic of many neurotic and nearly neurotic people. Successful people sometimes do not exhibit their self-defeating behavior in a significant way until they are close to achieving or have achieved some major goal. As the climax to a hard-won victory is about to be achieved, they spoil it for themselves and often for other people.

Management Consultant. Marvin, a onetime management consultant, had many times in the past ruined things for himself just as he was on the brink of success. A junior consultant who worked on Marvin's team describes how Marvin's self-defeating behavior surfaced on one important occasion:

Our team had done an extensive study of the marketing potential for indoor-outdoor carpeting for a client. We had done such a good job at the division level that we were invited to make a presentation to the top management team, with a likely outcome that we would be invited to conduct similar studies for other new products. Five company executives and two of us were gathered in the conference room near the president's office. The only person absent from the meeting was Marvin. A half-hour later we heard the voice of a person singing

coming from the corridor. Marvin entered the conference room in denims, calf-high boots, and he was carry-
ing a motorcycle helmet. His clothing was splattered
with mud (it had been raining that morning), and he
was absolutely stoned on grass. I'm not so sure the
executives knew what Marvin was smoking, but they
weren't good-natured about it.

I tried to quiet Marvin down and make the report myself, even though I was only prepared to give back-up
information. The meeting turned into a fiasco. After
about 20 minutes, the president said politely: "Thank
you, gentlemen. I think we have heard enough. Just forward us your written report. Thanks for your efforts."
When Marvin returned to normal behavior the next day,
all he could do was apologize. It was apparent the guy
wanted to fail. Too bad he dragged us down with him.

Aberrant behavior in management sometimes stems from
another variety of self-defeating behavior—the wish to be
punished. People occasionally violate rules, customs, or
laws with the unconscious intention of being caught. A
woman from Boston described to me the deviant behavior of
a manager, which suggests the machinations of somebody
who wants to lose his job:

Jerry was well known to the experienced women in
the office as a person who held out false promises in exchange for a little extramarital companionship. With
great predictability he would have an affair with some
underling, usually a naive secretary who wanted to become an assistant. After about a three-month affair, the
girl involved would be mysteriously transferred to the
steno pool or be asked to resign. She would be given
some trumped-up reasons, such as the company was becoming overloaded with potential administrative assistants. If she would leave the company, according to Jerry, it would be the best thing for her career. In addition
to his warped sense of ethics, Jerry had a drinking problem. He himself was finally let go from the company.[9]

Executive Vice-President. Wolman observes from his clinical practice with executives and others that self-defeating behavior is so well disguised that it sometimes gives the impression of a rational course of action. Nathan Goren, the newly appointed executive vice-president of a small company, finally sought psychological help just short of losing his job. Wolman describes Goren's display of managerial deviancy.

> Mr. Goren was thrilled when he got the job of executive vice-president . . . and initially he displayed a good deal of vigor and initiative. He got new business for the company, hired a new public relations man, improved production practices, and reorganized the accounting department. Everybody was pleased with Mr. Goren's zeal, initiative, perceptiveness, and vigor.
>
> The honeymoon on the new job did not last very long. Nathan Goren was a divorced man and dated frequently, but knew very well not to mix his personal life with his business responsibilities. Still, although he gave fatherly advice to one of the younger executives, he himself managed to get involved with his pretty and ambitious secretary. In no time he alienated his coworkers by promoting his secretary to a senior and undeserved position; after awhile his office turned into a hornet's nest of intrigues and counterintrigues. Angry factions of men and women sabotaged each other's work, causing a decline in productivity. Mr. Goren tried to restore morale by firing several people and promoting those who played yes-man to him and won his favor, but his policy caused a further decline in efficiency; and the people who lost their jobs reported the entire affairs to Mr. Goren's superiors.[10]

Later Goren reflected: "But I am a master at making trouble for myself. I know that every time things go right, something wrong will happen. Sometimes I begin to worry as soon as I get something out of life. And there it is, bingo. Bad luck? Fortune? What's the matter with me?"

Hate, Anger, and Aggression

Human beings have many disguised and undisguised
negative feelings such as hate, anger, and aggression.
Disputes, conflict, and some forms of managerial deviancy
are a natural outgrowth of these feelings. In short, a manager
may behave in a deviant manner simply because his or her
extreme negative emotions are expressed in a work environment. A production control manager's description of his
boss in action illustrates this underlying dynamic in deviancy:

> I say Frank is bad news for a couple of reasons. Let
> me tell you how he intimidated our engineering manag-
> er, Al, in a staff meeting. After Al made his presentation
> on the development of a new product, Frank called him
> "Al the Albatross," saying that if the company went
> ahead with his wild schemes, it would soon be bank-
> rupt. Al looked sick to his stomach after that blast in
> front of the other members of the management team.
>
> Another time I asked to see Frank in private. He had
> been spearheading a big cost-cutting campaign. It was
> apparent to me that our people were being squeezed too
> hard. Frank had even suggested that we postpone some
> scheduled repainting of the shipping docks. There was
> also a curtailment on the purchase of minor items such
> as screwdrivers and wrenches. I told Frank about these
> problems and he replied: "I'm glad the troops are com-
> plaining. Let me know when you begin to see their
> blood from squeezing them too tight." Frank is really
> an angry executive. I wonder what he's like at home.

Pathological Family Patterns

The roots of some forms of managerial deviancy are deep.
An unhealthy, or pathological, family pattern in childhood
can contribute to the development of a personality structure
with a predisposition to deviance. Many managerial devi-

ants, however, were raised in healthy family environments and many nondeviant managers have been raised in pathological family situations. As one company president described his father's influence on his personal development, "My father taught me one important lesson about business. He was a perfect model of what not to do. I can still recall creditors coming to the house or telephoning, trying to pin down the whereabouts of my father. He wasn't a ruthless father, but he was a ruthless businessman. When he owned a used-car lot, he used to stuff rust holes on cars with a putty-like substance and then paint over the mess. He told me to assume everybody in business is dishonest until proven otherwise. He didn't even trust banks."

Deviant behavior among managers sometimes comes about as they relate to subordinates in the same inappropriate way their parents related to them. Among the faulty parent-child relationships that would also lead to faulty (if not deviant) superior-subordinate relationships are rejection, overprotection, domination, overpermissiveness, perfectionism with unreal demands, faulty discipline (too little, too much, or inconsistent), contradictory demands, and undesirable parental models.[11] Currently popular techniques for modifying human behavior, such as transactional analysis and behavior modification, reject the idea that the present must be blamed on the past. Nevertheless, for some people, early childhood relationships influence the present.

Research evidence along these lines comes from Stanley S. Guterman's analysis of Machiavellianism in organizational life. His findings generally support some Freudian ideas about the superego, whereby people adapt their moral codes from their parents' behavior. Machiavellianism, an amoral, manipulative attitude toward other people, shows a correlation with people's recollections of certain parental characteristics. "Thus the greater the rapport the respondent [in the study] had with his parents and the stricter they were, the less likely he is to be Machiavellian. Also, the more Machiavellian the respondent remembers his parents as having been, the more likely he is to be Machiavellian. . . ."[12]

Early Psychic Trauma

Under rare circumstances a manager or staff person may experience a situation at work that closely parallels a traumatic experience early in life. In defense against a reenactment of the early life trauma, the person may behave irrationally, and sometimes the irrational behavior is deviant behavior.

College Professor.   Stan badly wanted to become chairman of his department. His desire for this administrative position was heightened when the current chairman announced his forthcoming retirement. Recognizing that Peggy, a department member of equal rank and experience, represented his most serious competition, Stan launched a campaign to discredit Peggy's credentials. Among his naive maneuvers was to hint to two people that Peggy had faked the data for an experiment whose results had recently been published in a major scientific journal. Confronted by the department chairman and Peggy about the libel he had been committing, Stan sought help from a counselor in the student mental health services on campus. Relating this rivalry with Peggy to his childhood, he told the counselor:

> I could see all those angry feelings I had about my sister come to the surface again. One incident stands out in my mind, and I can't seem to shake it, no matter what I do. An uncle of ours lived in California, while we lived in Chicago. When he visited us one Christmas, he told my parents that whoever earned higher grades the next term would be given a prize of spending one month with him at his California home that summer. When grades were sent out, I learned I had a 93 average. I was so thrilled, I raced into my room and began to sort out my belongings for the California trip. An hour later my sister came home and showed us her report card. Her average was 95. At that moment, things seemed to black out. All I could think of was punching my sister. I remember telling my parents that she probably cheated on her final exams.

Prediction of Managerial Deviance

The ability to predict which people will become deviants before they are hired by an organization is of considerable practical value. In light of the costs and consequences of deviance summarized in the previous chapter, it is reasonable to conclude that the prediction of deviance is even an *urgent* matter. Predicting that a given candidate for a managerial position will or will not manifest deviant behavior on the job involves predicting that a person who was deviant in the past will be deviant again, and that a person who has not been deviant in the past will be deviant in the future.

In general, the best predictor of future behavior is past behavior. Thoroughly combing through a person's past job experiences to document any prior instances of deviancy is thus crucial. Former FBI agents are sometimes hired by executive search firms or industrial companies to carry out this type of investigation, particularly for top executive positions in industry and government. As thorough as these investigations seem, many instances of past deviancy often go unreported because few people are willing to risk being accused of libel by making statements such as, "Sure, I can tell you something negative about that vice-president you're considering. He lies, cheats, and steals. Don't trust him with money or people."

Predicting that a person has a predisposition to deviance and that under the right circumstances, this deviant behavior will surface, is difficult. Psychological evaluations conducted by experienced consultants are helpful but not foolproof. Psychological evaluation predictions about deviance are more likely to err on the side of leniency than to falsely impute deviant tendencies to an individual. Organizations often use psychological evaluations (interviews and testing conducted by a trained psychologist) to screen out emotionally unstable people and are dissatisfied when the evaluation fails to fulfill this purpose. While working as a junior member of a psychological consulting firm, I had the following experience.

Visiting a firm in Long Island to talk about reinstating a

candidate-selection program our firm had conducted for them in the past, I was granted an interview with the president. He said: "Look, I'm a little bit wary of you fellows. Once we sent you a candidate and the psychologist who evaluated him said the guy could practically walk on water. I never read such a positive evaluation. He proved to be one of the biggest 'rounders' we ever had on the payroll. Twice he went on three-day drunks. His wife once called my office, claiming that he was running around with one of our secretaries." Deviancy of any variety, including alcoholism, is difficult to predict, yet this company president may have been overreacting to one grossly inaccurate prediction.

Implications for Management Action

Do the ideas presented thus far imply that managerial deviancy stems from factors so ingrained that the course of deviancy can't be altered? No. My theoretical position is much more optimistic. The core assumption of my action plan for combating deviancy is that it is both ineffective and inefficient for a manager to attempt to change the motives or other internal states of a deviant individual. As will be described in later chapters, managerial deviancy can be managed without a manager attempting to reconstruct the personality of another.

The strategy for controlling deviant behavior in management involves four steps. First, the deviant individual is confronted with his or her deviant behavior and the implications of that behavior. Second, an action plan is developed for doing something constructive about altering that behavior, including setting target dates and using outside sources of help as needed. Third, a schedule is established of rewards for progress toward the goal of nondeviant behavior, combined, if necessary, with a schedule of punishments for deviant behavior. Fourth, a series of periodic review sessions are established, supplemented by spontaneous feedback sessions which serve as both a gauge of progress and a setting for additional confrontation.

4

Pressures Toward Deviance

Can an organization drive its members to deviant behavior?
Is it possible that an open, honest, ethical, and mentally
healthy manager with a 10-year record of nondeviancy will
suddenly become a managerial deviant under the wrong (or
right) organizational pressure? Perhaps the real issue is less
simple. A more appropriate conception of the relationship
between organizational pressures and individual deviancy
looks at two variables simultaneously. A person with a predisposition to deviant behavior may exhibit deviance under
certain stressful circumstances. Deviant behavior thus
reflects an interaction between a person and his environment. Under sufficiently adverse circumstances most people
will display deviant behavior if they feel that deviant behavior will help them cope with the situation at hand. Conversely, a small number of people will never exhibit deviant
behavior, even under the most adverse situations. This relationship between the individual deviancy and organizational pressures can be illustrated by the hypothetical situation
of George, an account executive in a market research firm.

George has an average predisposition to ethical deviancy.
Up to now he has shown signs of deviance only once—an
episode that occurred during college. Pressed for time because of a death in his family, George bought an essay from

a national "research company" to use as a term paper in a political science course. In his present situation, his boss has put considerable pressure on him to increase client billings. His company needs new accounts in order to avoid a serious retrenchment. One Monday morning George receives a telephone call from an executive inquiring about market research services. During a luncheon conference later that week, George learns the true nature of the services requested. The prospective client is willing to pay a large sum of money to learn some intimate technical details about a new product development of a certain company. Predictably, that certain company is a present client of George's firm.

Under normal circumstances George would probably reject this proposal as a bribe to conduct corporate espionage. Under the present circumstances of his being pressured to increase billings, though, he might possibly rationalize this assignment as a highly confidential service that he would perform only in an unusual situation. Another account executive with a lesser predisposition to deviance would probably immediately reject this offer as a flagrant violation of business ethics. In this chapter we examine a variety of organizational pressures that lead some people—mostly those with a predisposition to such behavior—into managerial deviance.

Organizational Captives

Blair suffers the plight of thousands of middle managers in American companies. After 15 years of experience with his company, he has been passed over for the vice-presidency level for the last time. Little hope exists for Blair to achieve his ambition of becoming an executive in his company, yet his performance is not poor enough for him to be fired. His position seems almost like make-work to him, yet he sees limited job opportunities for himself in other companies. Few jobs for middle managers of ordinary accomplishment can be found in the economy of the mid-1970s. His above-average income and benefits, combined with his lack of mobility, make him an organizational captive.

Although no company will make a public statement that they have a deliberate policy of creating "shelf-sitters," the *overaccumulation of management resources* has become a widespread problem in business and industry. According to Samuel R. Connor and John S. Fielden, writing for the *Harvard Business Review,* the number of shelf-sitters in large corporations has increased three to five times since the early 1950s. "As U.S. industrial corporations have grown more complex, the number of middle managers has increased faster than has either the worker or the top-management population."[1] Human resource planners in large industries have recently begun to call this phenomenon the "middle management mushroom."

Deviant behavior in response to being an organizational captive is the end point on a continuum that begins with concern and goes through frustration to deviance. William Constandse observes that people who have become stuck in their jobs create a high-priority personnel management problem, "since they are understandably less motivated than the younger generation who still have confidence in themselves and the future. As a result, they are likely to be less productive and may develop such negative attitudes that they adversely affect the morale of the employees in their departments."[2]

Aware that they are vulnerable to layoff because top management considers them deadwood, they exhibit signs of deviancy of indecision by *playing it safe.* Constandse notes further: "They do this by writing weasel-worded memoranda, sharing responsibility through management by committee, and referring any formally proposed innovation that tends to 'rock the boat' to a study group, with the hope that it will die a natural death there."[3]

Executive AWOLism, a form of unauthorized absenteeism, is one form of deviancy directly precipitated by the uncomfortable pressures of having a meaningless job to perform. Few people who have not experienced the discomfort of being forced to appear constructively busy while having limited actual work to perform will be able to empathize with the managerial shelf-sitter. For some managers, the pangs of guilt from attending a matinee are less disquieting than having to sit in an office idling away time.

Inflexible retirement programs represent an eminently practical reason why many people remain with one organization despite the fact that they are occupying a shelf-sitter position.[4] One middle manager expressed his reasons for remaining with a company that no longer thought he had management potential: "If I can sweat it out another five years, I can get my retirement check and use it as a subsidy for setting up my own business." The Employee Retirement Income Security Act of 1974 may eventually decrease the number of instances in which managers cling to one company for fear of losing their retirement benefits. According to the provisions of this act, the labor force (including management) will have more clearly defined rights to pension funds. Should the day arrive when managers can transfer pension rights from one company to another, one more pressure toward deviancy will be lessened.

Misplacement of People

A decade ago Harry Levinson considered the misplacement of people to be a major factor underlying the maladaptive behavior of many managers.[5] Several years later, Laurence J. Peter and Raymond Hull came to national attention with *The Peter Principle*, an extension of the basic premise of personnel management that people promoted once too often tend to be ineffective.[6] Aside from creating problems for the organization, misplaced people are subject to considerable stress. A not unusual response to such stress is some form or forms of managerial deviancy. The pressure to perform in a position for which one is unsuited can bring to the surface predispositions to self-defeating, aberrant behavior.

A realization that some people succumb to deviant behavior in response to the pressure of misplacement helps illuminate the true meaning of job pressure. My observation is that *pressure* is a subjective feeling that occurs when a person lacks the necessary skills to cope with a given situation. Thus a tennis player or a sales manager does not experience significant pressure when the opposition is easy (that is, when he has the acquired skills to outperform the opposition).

Purchasing Manager. Rudy, a purchasing manager with five years of experience, was appointed manager of manufacturing in a company reshuffling. His boss, the person who misplaced Rudy, describes how Rudy became an *abdicator of authority.*

Agreed, it was my fault for throwing Rudy to the wolves in the first place. Our problem was common throughout the industry. We had a tremendous backlog of orders for our product. Due to the worldwide shortage of materials, our suppliers couldn't take good care of us and we couldn't take good care of our customers. Our top manufacturing man received a better offer and left. I figured this would be a good growth opportunity for Rudy, so we put him in charge of manufacturing.

Rudy's background in purchasing was helpful, but it wasn't good enough. He was just in over his head as the man in charge of manufacturing. He didn't know what the real problems were or how to solve the problems he did uncover. I first noticed Rudy wasn't holding up under the pressure when he would send the factory manager instead of himself to my staff meetings. At first he just brought the factory manager to the meetings to answer difficult questions, but then Rudy stopped coming to the staff meetings entirely. He had his secretary send my secretary a message with an excuse why he couldn't attend. The excuses didn't seem valid to me, so I investigated further. Just chatting with a few people, it became obvious that Rudy was ducking responsibility. The poor guy completely froze in the job. Now we have Rudy back in charge of purchasing in another division of the company, and he's doing fine. We have replaced him with a manufacturing pro who can handle the situation.

Exorbitant Work Demands

In contrast to the shelf-sitters described above, many managerial personnel are plagued with workloads that are beyond reasonable levels. Days crammed with meetings, heavy overnight travel, and simultaneous demands on one's time are some of the factors that make for exorbitant work demands. Stress of this kind is a factor that frequently underlies a manager resorting to alcohol and/or legal drugs as a palliative. Agitated by heavy workloads and long hours, a manager may find it culturally acceptable to use tranquillizers or whiskey as a way to calm down. Calmed down, but still facing a heavy workload, the same manager may rely on alcohol as a "bracer" for the day's responsibilities. Equally habituating are antidepressants which the same manager may resort to to energize himself when the amount of work to be performed seems onerous. Unfortunately, as a person increases his consumption of drugs and alcohol, he becomes less effective. Decreased effectiveness has the net effect of making the heavy workload seem all the more unmanageable.

Hotel Manager.   A man who went to his family doctor for help describes how his work situation led to his alcohol abuse (note again, however, that managerial deviance is an interaction between a predisposition to deviance and the stress imposed by the organization):

> Our hotel, located in what used to be the best downtown location, began to experience a downturn in business. Fewer businessmen coming to town wanted to stay with us because of the bad reputation our section of town had developed. A few well-publicized muggings, including one that involved the death of an executive by a streetwalker's pimp, really hurt the restaurant and hotel trade in our section of town.
>
> Headquarters told us that we had to cut personnel to compensate for declining business. Well, we did that and the personnel cuts just aggravated our business situation. As we cut people off our payroll, the quality of

our service declined. Because our reservation department was overloaded, more mistakes were being made in getting accommodations for people. Maintenance began to suffer. The dining room no longer had good service. As a result of declining business, we had to continue to reduce the payroll. The worse the service, the worse the business. Top management just wouldn't agree to taking a long shot on hiring back the right number of people and hoping that the improved service would bring business back to the hotel.

My personal workload about doubled, then almost tripled because of the reductions I had to make in my staff. I had to sacrifice two assistant hotel managers. My drinking problem began to take hold of me as I worked longer hours. Because of my fatigue and tension, I started having a drink at lunch to relax and maybe perk me up. As I worked more nights, I would have a couple of drinks before dinner and after I finished working late at night. Before I knew it, I was having a total of six drinks before I headed home at night. I finally went for help when my wife and boss told me in the same week that I was becoming an alcoholic.

Ambiguous, Amorphous Positions

People outside large, multilayered organizations are incredulous that some managers lack a clear conception of the nature of their jobs. However unlikely it sounds on logical grounds, many managerial and staff people experience *role ambiguity*—the condition that exists when a person has less than all the information he needs to accomplish a job. Role ambiguity has been comprehensively studied by organizational psychologists, Robert L. Kahn, John R. P. French, Jr., and Robert D. Caplan.[7] One of their conclusions is that uncertainty about one's job expectations can exert considerable stress.

Two studies about role ambiguity were carried out independently at different times and with different populations.

In the first study, 53 people from six large business organizations were interviewed about various aspects of stress and strain in their jobs. A major finding of this study was that ". . . men who suffered from role ambiguity experienced lower job satisfaction and higher job-related tension."[8] In the second study, conducted at Goddard Space Flight Center, 205 administrators, engineers, and scientists filled out a questionnaire describing various aspects of stress and related strain in their jobs. As part of the study, blood samples were taken and measures were made of blood pressure and pulse rate. A major finding was that role ambiguity was negatively associated with job satisfaction. Role ambiguity was positively associated with "feelings of job-related threat to one's mental and physical well-being." Another finding that bears on the stress created by role ambiguity was that "the more ambiguity the person reported, the lower was his utilization of his intellectual skills and knowledge ($r = -.48$), and the lower was his utilization of his administrative and leadership skills. This lack of utilization also adversely affected satisfaction and increased the job-related threat."[9]

What form of managerial deviancy tends to be associated with the stress of role ambiguity? As with any organizational source of stress described in this chapter, it is impossible to specify precise relationships between type of stress and type of deviancy. Furthermore, an individual's peculiar predisposition to deviancy would have to be known in order to make accurate predictions of this kind. With these limitations in mind, it is postulated that *preoccupation with busywork* is a mild form of managerial deviancy sometimes associated with acute cases of role ambiguity.[10]

Marketing Information Analyst. Fred resorted to busywork to cope with his ambiguous role, as reported by a personnel manager in his company:

> Fred had the misfortune to accept a job as a liaison man between marketing and management science. He was supposed to translate marketing questions into computer language. The other aspect of his job involved describing to marketing what computer science could

do for them. When the computer boys did come up with an analysis for marketing, it was Fred's job to help explain to marketing how these results could best be used. The whole job was kind of fuzzy. Fred described himself as an interface, or swing man, but he felt uncomfortable in that spot.

After awhile Fred stayed in his offices drawing up elaborate systems diagrams and flow charts. He began to read all the journal articles he could find about computer systems that applied to marketing. Maybe he sensed he wasn't needed, so he kept himself busy with projects nobody, not even he, cared about.

Impoverished Interpersonal Relationships

Adequate relationships between organizational members seems to be a necessary condition for organizational health. Organizations marked by extremely poor relationships among people create yet another form of stress that could precipitate deviant behavior among those people with pre-deviant personalities. Role ambiguity, as described above, is a major source of impoverished interpersonal relationships. French and Caplan note that misunderstandings and conflicts may occur where adequate information regarding roles and responsibilities (and the information necessary to carry them out) are not provided.[11] Conditions such as these lead to lowered trust and supportiveness among people, along with an increased reluctance to listen to each other's problems. Eventually poor interpersonal relationships of this nature produce dissatisfaction with the job and feelings of being threatened.

A more frequent form of impoverished relationships among organizational members is outright conflict between groups and people. Interpersonal or intergroup conflict can be waged at an intense level in many organizations. Frequently top management is unaware that dysfunctional conflict is taking place below them in the organization. When top management is aware of conflict at lower organizational levels, one or two unusual circumstances exist (often in tandem): (1) the organization may have naturally good channels of communication because most members trust each other; or (2) extensive use is made of behavioral science technology such as organization development meetings.

Mental Health Evaluation Team. Under the stress of prolonged and intense interpersonal conflict, some of the participants may behave irrationally or deviantly. Retaliation and revenge become more important than accomplishing tasks which serve the good of the organization as a whole. A recent example from the community mental health field illustrates how prolonged intergroup and interpersonal conflict can precipitate deviant behavior among people in responsible positions:

> An evaluation team was assigned to determine if community mental health services in a northeastern community were accomplishing their stated objectives of improving the mental health of those people receiving services. All team members, except for a liaison person with the agency, were hired as consultants to the state. The purpose of this organizational arrangement was to enhance the objectivity of their evaluation report.
>
> From the outset, the director of the evaluation team and the agency head clashed. The psychiatrist in charge of the agency accused a sociologist of being an "academic" with little understanding of the processes or purposes of clinical treatment methods. The sociologist, in turn, accused the psychiatrist of being practitioner-oriented, with little respect for the scientific method or hard data. After introducing the sociologist at a staff meeting, the psychiatrist told the group: "Let us all give R. and his team all the cooperation he needs. He has assured me that his academic experiments will not interfere with the treatment process." During a television interview about his activities, the sociologist said: "My role is one of evaluation, not of criticism. Before we can conclude that our community mental health service is any better for ill people than taking a warm bath or talk-

ing to their favorite bartender, we must obtain some conclusive evidence."

After the study had progressed several months, displays of deviance had been manifested on both sides of the intergroup conflict. The sociologist accused the psychiatrist of instructing his staff to coach clients and patients on how to respond to evaluation interviewer questions. According to the professor, people were told to exclaim how terrific they felt since making visits to the agency, and how "well integrated their lives had become." The psychiatrist had a countercharge. He claimed that the sociologist and his team were asking clients loaded questions such as "What concrete evidence do you have that your experiences at the center did you any good? Are you convinced that coming here has had any lasting benefit for you? Has your husband actually changed since his visit to the center?"

Job Insecurity

In years past, production and clerical workers were the first people to be laid off in times of business downturn. A new trend is for business, educational, and governmental organizations to decrease the number of middle managers and staff assistants when a reduction in forces becomes necessary. Many members of middle management and staff personnel recognize, in addition, that their organizations could continue to function effectively if they left and were not replaced. Peter Drucker states: "There is not one company I know of where a sharp cut in the number of executives wouldn't be a real improvement."[12]

Threats of losing one's job are thus sufficiently real to many managers and staff people to constitute another organizational pressure. Deviant responses to job insecurity tend to involve a variety of self-protective behaviors—all designed to increase a person's hold on his job.

Empire-building is a hazardous but widely practiced maneuver intended to make a person more powerful in the or-

ganization and therefore more job secure. So well known is
this practice that an exposition of its nature is superfluous.
An organization development consultant working full time
for a medium-sized conglomerate describes the informal diagnostic signs he uses to detect the empire-builder:

> I get the impression organizational paranoia and em-
> pire-building go hand in hand. The more worried a
> manager is that other people are out to get his job, the
> more likely he is to try and build a fortress of people
> around himself. What a person should do when he's
> worried about losing his job because he is becoming ex-
> cess is confront the problem and tell the company that
> he needs more work. He should do the same thing with
> his subordinates. Find honest work for them to do in
> the company.
> But instead the insecure guy looks for an "assistant
> to" to make himself seem more important in the organi-
> zation. Another sign is that the manager who wants to
> exaggerate his importance creates another layer of man-
> agement below himself. In his eyes, this makes his
> function doubly important. Another clue we get that a
> person is trying to build an empire is when a new posi-
> tion created under a manager has a nebulous job de-
> scription. *Real* jobs are easy to describe.

Extreme forms of deviancy in response to job insecurity
involve attempts to discredit other people who could pose a
serious threat to one's job. For instance, a manager worried
about a subordinate taking his job might try to find some
way of discrediting that subordinate. A branch manager in a
casualty insurance company exhibited deviant behavior
when asked about the promotability of the assistant branch
manager. Although in previous discussions he had spoken
quite highly of Jeff, he now had a contrary statement: "Jeff
looks pretty solid on the outside. He came up through sales
and was able to get by there with his appearance and charm.
But I know he really has no guts underneath. His lack of

self-confidence would be a real problem in a responsible job."

Note that if Jeff's manager believed that Jeff lacked self-confidence (even if his judgment were wrong) his behavior would not be classified as deviant. It is the deliberate distortion of truth in order to favor one's own position that must be categorized as deviancy.

Encouragement of Power-Seeking

"Grabs for power" can be explicit examples of deviant behavior, yet organizations encourage some degree of power-seeking. Presumably organizations are often unaware that the encouragement of power-seeking may lead to devious maneuvers to attain additional power. Harry Levinson presents a penetrating analysis of the subtle process by which power-seeking is encouraged. Central to his thesis is that power-oriented personal characteristics are rewarded by the organization:

> No single kind of subordinate pleases his superiors more than the man who is able to assume responsibility for a crisis task, jump to his task with zest, and accomplish it successfully with dispatch. Such men become the "jets" of industry, and the "comers," the "shining lights." They are usually bright, energetic managers who have considerable ability and even more promise. . . .
>
> Naturally, higher management rewards such men for their capacity to organize, drive, and get results. Management therefore encourages them in their wide-ranging pursuit of personal power. . . .[13]

Power-seeking is built into the structure of any hierarchical organization, thus encouraging deviance in any manager so predisposed. In the culture of the organization, more responsibility is considered better than less responsibility,

more subordinates is better than fewer subordinates, high
salary is better than low salary, and more responsibility
means more money. In most organizations, "large numbers
of managers are competing for a small number of openings
available at the top of the organizational pyramid."[14]

Power-seeking among managers only becomes aberrant
behavior when (a) the means of acquiring power are immoral, and/or (b) power is sought for the good of the individual
only, rather than for the good of the organization. Assume
that a college administrator attempts to achieve power by increasing the student enrollment. He goes about his power
grab in a sensible manner by applying techniques of marketing to higher education (for instance, he conducts a community survey about their educational requirements).[15] The
end result of his power grab is that the college is financially
sounder and the community has been better served. Financial rewards are forthcoming to the college administrator,
but he has achieved them in an ethical and constructive
manner.

Account Executive.   Power-seeking sometimes involves
more devious means and ends. Joan sought power beyond
her account executive position in an advertising agency. Her
approach to gaining additional power was to attempt to
confine her work to successful clients, while simultaneously
getting clients with less potential for success assigned to
other account executives. Eventually her superior, Blaine,
caught onto her machinations and confronted her about the
problem. Blaine describes one of Joan's maneuvers:

> I don't know why it took me so long to figure out what
> Joan was up to. Her approach was very similar to the
> psychoanalyst who reports all kinds of great cures. The
> problem is, he only takes on patients who are well and
> don't really require treatment; just a sympathetic ear.
> Joan would make up legitimate-sounding reasons why a
> particular client was better suited for another account
> executive. Her favorite line was: "Harriet's personality
> will mesh with that client, while mine will clash" or:
> "If we are truly concerned with the southeast quadrant

of the balance sheet, let's assign the right people to the right accounts." What Joan really meant was that the product to be advertised for that client looked like a loser. As we know all too well in this business, no advertising campaign can stop customers from returning junk products to the retailers. Joan wanted to get her tentacles on a winning product. Lying to get there didn't bother her.

Deviancy at the Summit

Perhaps the most subtle, yet the most influential, pressure toward deviance in an organization is deviant behavior on the part of top management. Top management's behavior serves as a model for lower levels of management. People follow models, among other reasons, because it is tacitly assumed that leaders *want* followers. Deviant behavior at the top of an organization is rarely kept secret. Organizational members at lower levels therefore do not have to be told explicitly what kind of behavior is truly encouraged. When the company is being sued for back taxes, it is not unusual that middle managers and sales personnel will inflate expense accounts. When the chairman of the board works only three hours a day (and with most of that time devoted to reading newspapers), it is not unfathomable that junior executives work on their income tax returns during working hours.

Ethical and value deviancy is more profoundly influenced by top management behavior than are personal habits. For example, although a company owner is known to be an alcoholic, few subordinates will adopt this pattern of maladaptive behavior because of the owner's addiction. Extreme departures from a *reasonable* code of ethics are considered deviance within the framework of this book. Ethical deviants thus include the food-processing manager who simply "crosses his fingers and hopes for the best" when the quality control department discovers that a few rat pellets may be in one shipment of food, the landlord who forges signatures and cashes his welfare tenants' checks, and the college dean who encourages students to enroll in a program of study for an obsolete field.

What is a reasonable code of ethical executive behavior? Robert Austin has established ground rules for executive conduct that are useful as a rough standard of nondeviant behavior:

1. The professional business manager affirms that he will place the interests of the business for which he works before his private interests.

2. The professional business manager affirms that he will place his duty to society above his duty to his company and above his private interest.

3. The professional business manager affirms that he has a duty to reveal the facts in any situation where (a) his private interests are involved with those of his company, or (b) where the interests of his company are involved with those of the society in which it operates.[16]

Radical departures from codes of conduct such as these constitute both ethical violations and organizational pressures toward deviance.

5

Confronting Deviant Behavior

Confrontation is the bedrock on which a workable system of deviance control is constructed. Abating or eliminating aberrant behavior in management inevitably involves another person—presumably the deviant's immediate superior—confronting the deviant with his or her behavior and its consequences. Confrontation is thus an essential ingredient to combating managerial deviance. The manager with a deviant subordinate must communicate clearly to the subordinate what it is about his behavior that significantly departs from acceptable behavior in that particular organization (or society in general). Unless this confrontation is conducted effectively, a vital early step in the control of deviance has been mismanaged. Despite the importance of confrontation in the management of deviance and other behavior problems, it is a skill rarely well developed by managers.

Why Managers Dislike Confrontation

It appears that the majority of managers dislike confronting subordinates about negative aspects of their performance or behavior. Many managers, even in role-playing exercises, become visibly uncomfortable (squirming, rapid foot-shuffling, and the like) when it is their turn to confront a subordinate with bad news. In contrast, most managers and staff people welcome the chance to play the role of the manager who has *good news* to communicate to a subordinate. For most of us, confrontation is not a comfortable experience, and the discomfort increases geometrically with the gravity of the confrontation. One vice-president of marketing talked about his plans to ask one of his product managers to resign:

> Good God, this is something I really hate to do. Mark isn't really a bad guy. He has had so many problems at home with his wife, that I don't think all his time away from work and his drinking have been entirely his fault. It just eats away at my guts to have to let a person go who has been with us for seven years. We've talked about his problems before, but this news will hit him like a bombshell. I wish there were a good time to tell people news like this.

Managers resist confronting subordinates for one or more of at least four different reasons, all of which seem valid to the manager at the time. Nevertheless, deviant behavior in organizations cannot be brought under control until this resistance to confrontation is recognized and overcome. Fortunately, acquiring insight into why you resist confrontation (assuming you have at least average control over your own behavior) can lead to overcoming the resistance.

A fundamental reason why we resist confronting another person, particularly a subordinate, about a sensitive issue is that we recognize how uncomfortable *we* feel when confronted by a boss about a sensitive issue. Many managers preconsciously say to themselves before confronting a subordinate about irregularities on an expense account: "I know how bad I would feel if I were told by my boss that I had been overcharging the company on trips. Maybe if I let it pass one more time, Carol [the subordinate] will shape up by herself."

Most people can recall the discomfort they experienced

the first time they were confronted about something that dealt with their basic character structure. Being confronted about job-related technical problems is much less uncomfortable. Should an accountant be confronted with the fact that he miscalculated the cost of a product his company manufactured, he can depersonalize this mistake. Should that same accountant be accused of preparing income tax forms for company employees during working hours, he will probably personalize that criticism as a negative comment about his character.

Fear of reprisals by the confronted person underlies the resistance of some managers to confronting the deviant behavior of a subordinate. What specific kind of reprisal might be chosen by the confronted subordinate (should the roles be reversed) is usually unknown, which makes the confrontation seem all the more hazardous. An aphorism emerging from some fast-growing organizations covers the contingency of extreme reprisal: *Never be unkind to a subordinate. He may become your boss within the year.*

The more powerful the subordinate to be confronted (or the more counterinformation he or she might have on you), the greater the fear of reprisal. A manager cannot readily threaten to report the expense account indiscretions of a subordinate to a higher management if the superior is aware that the subordinate has adverse information about him. Perhaps the subordinate is aware that the superior entertains friends with expense account money. Powerful subordinates—those who have informal alliances with members of top management—are in an advantageous position to exercise reprisals. A manager in an aerospace company was aware that one of his subordinates spent a good deal of time and money on ceremonial tasks such as visiting foreign customers. Although he felt this subordinate was "excess baggage," he hesitated to make a case for the subordinate's dismissal. The foreign traveler was a close personal friend of the president who had been hired many years before the arrival of his new boss.

Hospital Managers. A social worker describes an interesting reprisal that took place in a mental hospital:

Chris, the hospital head, had uncovered some really psychopathic behavior on the part of Don, the head of food services. Problems surfaced when the complaints about the quality of food became unusually frequent and forceful. Chris investigated and discovered that Don had a fairly healthy food budget. Further investigation revealed that Don had a manipulative arrangement with two of his wholesale food suppliers.

They would write up receipts for normal food deliveries, with normal prices. However, they would deliver a much poorer quality and less quantity of food. Don would get a kickback on the money paid to the supplier by the hospital. He would make a few dollars, but the patients would suffer. They would have to eat some bad, makeshift meals. Hamburger patties, for instance, were discovered to consist mostly of oatmeal.

Chris finally confronted Don about these irregularities. Don apparently had some very effective counterstrategy. He told Chris he wasn't the only trickster around the hospital. According to information Don had gathered, Chris had a few psychiatrists listed on the hospital staff who, in fact, spent about one afternoon a month on the premises. What Chris learned in a hurry was that one psychopath shouldn't confront another.

Another reprisal sometimes feared is that a confronted subordinate will deny the charges made against him or her and furthermore contend that the alleged charges are libelous. (Readers concerned about this type of reprisal would do well to document instances of deviant behavior by a subordinate.) Confrontation for this and other reasons explained in this chapter should deal with specific aspects of behavior. For instance, a manager should not be confronted with the observation that he is a *racist*. A more constructive approach is to confront that same manager with instances in which he practiced antiblack discrimination.

Management Consultant. To avoid (or minimize) the reprisal of being accused of libel, it is safest to confront people about observable aspects of behavior. The branch man-

ager of a consulting firm noticed that one of the junior consultants in his office had consistently recorded a low level of
client billing, yet was frequently out of the office. His
monthly progress reports were quite vague about any attempts to develop new clients. For this reason and a few in-
ferences based on statements made by the junior consultant,
the branch manager confronted him:

> "Marty, it appears to me you have been spending our
> time working on some future venture of your own. If
> you intend to go into business for yourself, quit now. It
> does our firm no good at all for you to be hustling new
> business on our time." Marty denied that this was the
> case and sent a letter to his boss later that week which
> included this statement: "I would prefer that you with-
> draw the negative statements made about me. Your ob-
> servations are untrue, and perhaps libelous. I am think-
> ing about handing this matter over to my attorney.

Managers and other people often resist confrontation because they feel unequal to the task of dealing with another
person's anger and hostility. Confrontation frequently leads
to an outburst of emotion by the person confronted. Many
people feel acutely uncomfortable when dealing with the
wrath of another person. One manager participating in a discussion group about problem employees said he would never tell an alcoholic that the reason for his dismissal was alcoholism. When another member of the group asked why,
the manager said: "Suppose the alcoholic got mad right in
my office. Then what would I do?"

Few managers fear that the deviant will physically strike
them in anger. What is feared is the awkwardness of handling undisguised anger in an environment where true feelings are usually disguised. Many managers and staff people
who have little difficulty expressing true anger to family
members (and receiving anger from them) find it difficult to
handle the same feelings on the job. A reluctance to handle
anger is not an irrational sentiment. Anger by another person generally makes the recipient tense if not angry himself.

Resentment, similar to anger, is often expressed from the person being confronted. A plant manager confronted with the observation that he was continuing to pollute the main river in town despite warnings to correct the situation, strongly resented being labeled a *reckless polluter.* He expressed his resentment this way: "This is typical of the treatment a plant manager gets around here. You staff executives are paid twice as much as we are for doing half the work. You place unbelievable pressure on us to run at a profit, yet you won't let us take care of the environmental problems out of your budget."

Concern about the consequences to the subordinate of being confronted with deviant behavior is another reason some managers prefer to avoid confrontation. "Suppose word gets out that the reason we had to demote Brad was his gambling. What will happen to his career?" This type of sentiment shows concern for the consequences to the person being confronted. The flaw in such reasoning is apparent: confronting a manager early about his deviant behavior may have less negative consequences to his career than a confrontation that takes place much later. Deviant behavior is best dealt with before its effects multiply. Many experienced managers have said that the kindest thing they could have done for an alcoholic subordinate would have been to let him know right away that he was on the way to losing his job. Confrontation can do more long-range good for an individual than the short-range good derived from denying a problem.

Another negative consequence to an individual from confrontation that is sometimes feared by a manager is that the person might "freak out." One executive expressed his apprehension this way: "If I tell him that I think he's really just a deadbeat who should no longer be on the payroll, he might mentally collapse. I've heard of things like that happening in sensitivity training." True, which kind of stress will precipitate which emotional reaction in another person can never be predicted with certainty. We know, however, that confrontation about job behavior, rather than about personal characteristics or motives (for example, calling someone a deadbeat) is less likely to be harmful to mental health. The subject of expressing confrontations about deviance into job-related behavior will be discussed later in this chapter.

Discovery and Detection

Discovery and detection of deviant behavior must logically precede confrontation. Detection and discovery take place in one of two ways. The person in charge of an organization, or a portion thereof, must have good communication channels or good powers of observation. People reporting to the deviant manager or his colleagues must tell that manager's superior about the deviant behavior he displays. In other situations the manager simply has to be sensitive to (observant of) deviance taking place close to him.

Top executives are often remarkably insulated from important events taking place below them in the organization. When the president of a food-processing firm finally learned that a key subordinate's promiscuity was disruptive to the company, he bemoaned: "Why didn't somebody tell me this was happening?" (One reason, unknown to the president, was that other executives thought the aberrant executive was a close personal friend of the president's.) In his classic article, "Clear Communications for Chief Executives," Robert N. McMurry describes how unaware many top executives are of crucial matters concerning their subordinates. He notes:

> Not only are many top executives unaware of what transpires within their organizations; they are even less well informed concerning the competence and potential of their key personnel. . . .
>
> Much of the operating inefficiency and internecine strife that plague many firms arises in part from the top manager's failure to be properly apprised of what is actually taking place in the organization. Often he knows neither how well suited each member of top, middle,

and first-line management is to his job assignment nor
the nature and extent of the consequences of his subordinate's maladaptation to his job where this exists.[1]

In short, unless an executive of an organization has
smoothly functioning communication channels between
himself and those immediately below him, he may remain
unaware of managerial deviance until the situation enters a
crisis stage. One president averted a crisis that could have
put his company out of business by maintaining open communication channels between himself and subordinates at
different levels in the organization.

Laboratory Owner. Mel, the owner of a small medical
laboratory that conducted diagnostic tests for physicians,
periodically toured his laboratory to conduct informal prob-
lem-gathering conferences. One day the routine question
asked of his production manager—"How are things going,
Sal?"—revealed deviant conduct that might have permanently ruined the reputation of the laboratory. Sal replied:
"Things are going pretty well, Mel, but I'm concerned about
one thing. Our revenues have been much too high lately for
the actual amount of tests we've been running. I get the aw-
ful feeling that somebody—and I'm not pointing a finger at
anybody in particular—is sending back blood and urine
analyses without actually having conducted tests. Maybe
you might want to check out this situation for yourself,
Mel."

Mel conducted a brief investigation which revealed that
laboratory tests *were* being faked and that the faked analyses
were being accompanied by negative reports (no disease or
abnormality found) which were sent back to private physicians. Because the proportion of diseased samples is so low,
this deception could conceivably have persisted for many
months without complaints from physicians or patients.

Alcohol and Drug Abusers. Deviancy related to alcohol
and drug abuse presents another set of considerations. Here
the problem of detection and discovery is the direct responsibility of the problem individual's immediate superior.
Careful observation of changes in behavior, followed by

confrontation, are the vital first steps in bringing about changes in behavior. Few managers who confront the problem have difficulty recognizing alcohol abuse in a subordinate, especially in the later stages of alcoholism. Behavioral changes occurring in earlier stages are more subtle; thus they deserve mention here, if only for review. Variations can be expected in individual cases, but the following list contains the more common signs managerial personnel with drinking problems may exhibit. All are observable by an immediate superior.

Occasional and poorly explained lapses in fulfilling responsibilities.

Occasional spasmodic work pace and, at times, unusually high work output on the part of a previously steady employee.

Minor decline in overall work quality or quantity, followed shortly by more pronounced decline.

Increased tendency to attempt to present self in a favorable light to superiors.

Marked improvement, or some deterioration in personal grooming, dress, and demeanor.

More pronounced spasmodic changes in work pace. Superior finds himself tending to report employee's performance level almost entirely on basis of peak periods.

More elaborate alibis for work deficiencies.

Personal appearance occasionally sloppy. Hangovers on the job.

Longer lunch periods. Fellow employees sometimes comment: "He drinks a bit too much."

Some evidence of financial problems.

Occasional off-the-job accidents or being arrested for driving while drinking.[2]

Drug dependence is a less familiar maladaptive behavior pattern to most management personnel than is alcohol dependence. Warning signs that a person is drug dependent vary somewhat from drug to drug (and from person to person); but there are some general signs of addiction that are useful in uncovering the drug abuser. Jordan M. Scher, executive director of the National Council on Drug Abuse, offers a word of caution about overinterpreting all possible signs of drug abuse: "It should also be remembered that a person may have a legitimate reason for possessing a syringe and needle (a diabetic), for possession of tablets and capsules (prescribed by a physician), having the sniffles and running eyes (a head cold or allergy), unusual or odd behavior (a true psychosis), etc."[3] Here is a list of common drug-abuse symptoms that could apply to managerial personnel:

Changes in attendance and discipline.

Change in the performance of the employee's normal capabilities.

Unusual flare-ups or outbreaks of temper.

Poor physical appearance, including inattention to dress and personal hygiene.

Wearing of sunglasses at inappropriate times to hide dilated or constricted pupils.

Long-sleeve shirts worn constantly to hide needle marks (only applicable in those rare organizations where the majority of managerial personnel wear short-sleeve shirts).

Attempting to obtain frequent salary advances.

Frequent reporting of unusually high expense account vouchers.

Finding the employee in odd places during normal working hours, such as closets and storage rooms, and excessive time in lavatory.[4]

Helpful Confrontation Techniques

Confrontation follows discovery and detection. At this stage many managers feel awkward and uncomfortable. Here the manager must confront the suspected deviant with the observation (and sometimes fact) that he or she is exhibiting maladaptive, dysfunctional behavior on the job. Few managers feel unequal to the task of scheduling a meeting with the managerial deviant to discuss his behavior. More difficult is thinking of an opening comment that will set the stage for the conversation to follow. Three general suggestions for beginning the meeting will be made first.

As difficult as it may seem, attempt to relax. If you appear overly tense, you might communicate the message in body language that you are not confident of the position you are taking about the person's maladaptive behavior. Perhaps a role-playing or rehearsal interview with a person from the personnel department (or outside the company) will be helpful in reducing your tension about the interview.

Getting to the central purpose of the meeting almost immediately is strongly recommended. Too often managers attempting to confront a subordinate about something sensitive waste time talking about peripheral topics. Discussions about vacations, the company parking lot, professional sports, or business conditions have some small value as warm-up material for *other* kinds of interviews, but that's all. The gravity of the matter to be discussed should be communicated during the first few minutes of the interview.

Avoid being apologetic or defensive about the need for the meeting. Every organization has a responsibility both to the outsiders it serves and to itself, to combat deviant behavior. For instance, there is no need to say, "Perhaps it's a case of mistaken identity, but word has gotten back to me that you have been taking orders for your furniture business during normal working hours." Let the suspected deviant correct you if the situation is a case of mistaken identity.

Confrontations about deviance should be conducted in a private, quiet office with no interruptions allowed. Managers sometimes feel more comfortable talking about sensitive matters over dinner or lunch. Conducting such a meeting on company time, on company premises, goes a long way toward eliminating the possible role confusion between the manager as a friend and the manager as a spokesman for the company. Discussions about important topics conducted in restaurants are sometimes interpreted as merely "friendly warnings."

With these general principles as a guideline, here are some sample opening statements for confrontation interviews:

> Marketing vice-president to product planner: "Word has gotten back to me that you are discussing our new product developments with competitors on a consulting basis. Let's talk about this situation."
>
> President to administrative assistant: "I've set up this interview to talk about your drinking problem. I regard it as very serious."
>
> High school principal to history teacher: "Several parents have complained to me that you have asked their daughters for dates. Let's get to the bottom of this problem."
>
> Controller to field auditor: "Your travel expenses for the last two months have been unrealistically high. Tell me about what's happening."
>
> Accounts payable supervisor to junior accountant: "There's something we must talk about. You give many signs of having a drug problem. Tell me about it."
>
> Company president to vice-president of finance: "I've asked you here for a very important purpose. We tell our stockholders that they must do what they can to fight inflation. We tell the labor union that their demands for

a wage increase are inflationary. And now you're urging us to increase prices 8.8 percent. I call that irresponsible. Explain it to me."

Vice-president of manufacturing to plant manager: "We have something very serious to talk about in relation to your employment practices. You're the only plant manager who has only white people in supervisory positions. Could you explain why this is so?"

Department head to college professor: "I have a major problem to discuss with you. At least a dozen students have complained to me that you have no interest in teaching. Your record suggests you also have no interest in research or writing. How do you see the problem?"

Hospital administrator to resident in internal medicine: "What I want to talk about is the fact that you are encouraging drug abuse. I recognize that you identify with the youth culture, but I have evidence that you are indiscriminately prescribing drugs for young people. I regard this as a prostitution of your profession. Let's talk about it."

Congressman to speechwriter: "I want to talk to you about a grave situation. I'm beginning to suspect your sense of ethics. Three times now you have suggested that I present a different viewpoint on the same issue to different segments of the population. Do you have a consistent set of beliefs?"

Construction company executive to salesman: "I have to talk to you about a serious violation of business ethics. You have sent in a construction bid on a condominium development without mentioning that our company can only build at this price if we use a considerable amount of scrap lumber. What else have you done of a similar nature?"

Hostile and Nonhostile Confrontation

Confrontations with subordinates about deviant behavior should be conducted with feeling (particularly sincerity), but not with hostility. Confrontations are associated with bitter conflict so frequently that the concept of confrontation connotes hostility. Yet all forms of confrontation need not be conflagrations.

A general principle for bringing about changes in behavior is for the confronter to confront in a nonhostile fashion. Hostility begets hostility. Most people become defensive when confronted hostilely. Confrontation mixed with hostility comes across to the person being confronted as an attempt at retribution or punishment. Although punishment is the appropriate motivator for some people in some situations, it should be regarded as a secondary recourse. Use positive motivators before you resort to negative motivators.

Nonhostile confrontation (the use of *friendly* confrontation would be extending the principle too far) attempts to place the problem of managerial deviancy on a problem-solving basis. Hostile confrontation is directed more toward accusation and the assigning of blame; it is also a mild form of *getting even* with the confronted person for his deviant behavior. Nonhostile confrontation usually sets the stage for solving a major problem faced by the individual and the organization: the modification of that person's deviant behavior.

What about all other negative emotion and feelings? Should they be ruled out of the confrontation session? No. An appropriate amount of displeasure, annoyance, disappointment, and controlled anger should be conveyed. A confrontation session stripped of legitimate feeling would appear sterile to the person confronted. Furthermore, even though I have carefully avoided the term *discipline* so far in our discussion of modifying aberrant behavior in management, many people, when confronted with their deviant behavior, will associate the confrontation interview with the disciplining they received earlier in life. For these people, authentic discipline is associated with some degree of angry feelings being displayed by the person administering the discipline.

Quality Control Manager. Haim G. Ginott, the late child and adolescent psychologist, has laid down rules for constructive criticism of adolescents by parents that are applicable to the present discussion.[5] Criticism, or confrontation, is most likely to be effective (to change behavior) when these principles are followed: (1) don't attack personality traits; (2) don't criticize character traits; and (3) deal with the situation at hand. When these principles are followed, the confrontation session will communicate less hostility than when they are violated. Here is how these suggestions might be applied to a confrontation between a manufacturing manager, Alex, and his quality control manager, Ken.

Alex has learned that Ken has ordered his people to skip some of their prescribed testing procedures for brake shoe linings because his department has fallen behind schedule. Ken reasons that so few of the parts are defective that customers will never catch the mistake. By omitting a few inspections, Ken and his department can reach their productivity goal. Alex has called Ken into his office for the first confrontation about this problem.

Alex might fall into the natural error of immediately attacking Ken's personality. For example: "Ken, if you weren't so *insecure* about your career, you would never have done anything as stupid as this." Ken would immediately become defensive about being labeled insecure and stupid. A psychologically sounder approach (following the tenets of Ginott) would be to criticize the *error:* "Ken, you have done something that could drive our company out of business and perhaps kill a few innocent people in the process. If word got out in the industry that we were shortchanging people on brake-lining inspections, we'd never get another contract."

Another trap into which Alex might easily fall is to criticize Ken's character traits. (Many might argue that an inadequate character structure is one major factor underlying deviant behavior, that deviancy is a character defect.) "Ken, what you have done is the *coward's* way out. Only a person without a *conscience* would do something like this. If you had enough guts to face the consequences of being behind schedule, you would never have ordered your people to skip those inspections." Nobody—not even a managerial deviant—wants to be called a coward without a conscience. Almost reflexively, Ken will look for ways to defend his character and perhaps levy countercharges against Alex and the company.

Alex must also realize that, aside from dealing with the errant behavior of his quality control manager, he is also dealing with an important business problem—the situation at hand. If Ken is to be rehabilitated and the problem solved, attention must also be focused on the present situation. Of additional value, focusing on the situation at hand helps the person who has committed the deviant act recognize the consequences of his behavior. Part of Alex's confrontation should involve a look at the consequences of omitting the inspections. "Our company is in a real mess now. Perhaps 10,000 brake linings have gone out the door without adequate inspection. Some of them must already be in the hands of parts wholesalers. We would need a massive recall. Some of the linings would be difficult to locate because of our complicated distribution system. We have to act fast to avoid a catastrophe." Attacking the situation in this manner will effectively communicate to Ken the gravity of his deviant behavior.

Confront the Job-Related Behavior

The essential skill to be acquired in constructive confrontation is to translate deviant behavior into its job-related consequences. Once the central behavioristic orientation is accepted—that behavior is shaped by its consequences—the necessity for dealing with job-related behavior, rather than the mysterious "inner person," becomes apparent. Even psychoanalysis has met with limited success in changing the character of people. The manager who is attempting to change deviant behavior must be able to work with the managerial deviant in terms of what his deviant behavior is doing to the task, job, or organization. The counterdeviance strategy suggested here is designed to lower the probability that deviant behavior will repeat itself. A person who becomes less deviant (that is, commits fewer deviant acts) may or may not have undergone a change in character. Managers must work with observable behavior because it is all that is available to them in a work environment.

Translating managerial deviance into its job-related consequences is effective for another important reason. Once the translation is made from the internal states of an individual (slothfulness, greed, and so forth) to its behavioral consequences (mismanagement of money, misallocation of resources) the situation is placed on a problem-solving basis. Superiors and subordinates can jointly solve concrete problems much more readily than they can deal with attitudes, predispositions, and values. For instance, a hospital administrator may receive complaints from male patients that one of the ward doctors is making homosexual advances toward them. The hospital administrator and the gay physician can jointly examine this problem of patients complaining about the staff behavior and arrive at some clear-cut courses of action: "Further complaints by patients that you are making sexual overtures toward them will result in your dismissal." In contrast, it is not within the power, skill, ability, or province of the administrator to advise the physician: "You must become a heterosexual to hold your job here." An additional problem, of course, is that telling people to change their sexual orientation or a variety of other personal habits is often considered an infringement of their civil liberties.

Translating tendencies to managerial deviance into specific, observable acts of job-related behavior is a skill that improves with practice. The underlying skill is the acquisition of precision in thinking about the difference between deviant tendencies (which are mediating factors) and deviance (which is a specific behavior).

Management Developer. Paul, a director of management development, considers his management development specialist, Dennis, to be a managerial deviant. Here is how an interchange between Paul and a consultant, designed to help Paul establish behavioral objectives about managerial deviancy, might proceed.[6] Note that the actual making of plans for combating deviancy must be established jointly between the managerial deviant and his superior. At this point we are merely examining the thinking process involved in translating deviant characteristics into job-related behavior.

PAUL: I have a problem with Dennis, my management development specialist. He's kind of an unethical chameleon type.

CONSULTANT: An unethical chameleon type?

PAUL: Yes, the kind of guy who changes his shape to fit whatever vessel he's in at the moment. I notice it and I think management is beginning to notice it. It's quite apparent. I even overheard a joke about him in the cafeteria that was quite derogatory.

CONSULTANT: In what way would you like him to change?

PAUL: I want Dennis to become less of a manipulating, two-faced staff member. His little tricks will soon backfire and our department will lose its good reputation. Then before long, our budget will be cut.

CONSULTANT: What specific changes do you want Dennis to make?

PAUL: Just what I said. Stop being a chameleon. Stop manipulating, stop being two-faced, stop being so slippery.

CONSULTANT: Still, you're being too general. The labels you use for Dennis may be accurate, but you're not tying them to specific job-related actions.

PAUL: Okay, try this one. Dennis has a strong tendency to tell management what they want to hear, whether or not he believes it himself.

CONSULTANT: Now you're getting there, but we still don't have a specific behavioral objective. Just take that one step further. Give an example.

PAUL: Here's one. Dennis is a well-educated person in his field. He believes strongly in grounding whatever programs he offers management in some solid theory. He thinks that unless a management development program has a good theoretical foundation, it won't be of lasting benefit to management. He has given a few talks to this effect. Then he found out that most members of management dislike theory. For some reason they think theory is impractical. So in his new proposal for a management development program, Dennis makes this statement on the introductory letter: "We know that management doesn't want a bunch of theory. So we have designed a real practical program." His letter nauseated me.

CONSULTANT: Now you've hit on a specific aspect of Dennis's deviant behavior. See if he'll agree to not put in writing things he doesn't believe to be true. Any other specific aspects of deviant behavior you can recall?

PAUL: I get the point. How about this one? Recently Dennis told the president that his speech was terrific. Later that same day he told the vice-president of finance that the president bombed out in his talk. A behavioral objective here would be for Dennis to be consistent in expressing his true opinion about company topics.

Readers who have worked under a management-by-objectives system will find familiar the process of establishing job-related behavioral objectives for deviance. For additional practice in translating deviant characteristics into job-related behavior, I have compiled a list of 10 kinds of managerial deviance, paired with one or more corresponding job-related behavioral objectives. It is important to recognize that any one form of deviance could conceivably result in numerous job-related behaviors that require change.

1. Kurt, a warehouse manager, is a compulsive gambler who makes frequent junkets to Las Vegas and returns depressed and distracted if his losses are substantial. His boss may not be able to help conquer Kurt's presumed need for self-punishment, but he can insist that even after "vacations," Kurt keep his department's shipping error down to 2 percent. His boss can also strongly recommend that Kurt join the local chapter of Gamblers Anonymous.

2. Martha, a drafting supervisor, has a drinking problem. Her boss cannot undo what her parents have done to her in childhood, but he can hold her accountable for regular attendance, seeking outside professional help for her drinking, and joining the local chapter of Alcoholics Anonymous.

3. Ira, a chief engineer, is forever fighting with someone in the organization. His manager can't help Ira overcome his inferiority feelings, but he can insist that Ira stop writing poison pen letters to other department heads, make no more unsupported accusations about the integrity of other company executives during staff meetings, and attend a conflict-resolution workshop given by a nearby management consultant, which is sponsored by the company.

4. Jackie, an account executive, is a malicious office politician. She tells lurid stories about other people in her advertising agency in an attempt to gain more power for herself. Her manager can't expect good results from telling Jackie to be more secure about her own capabilities, but he can admonish her: "Jackie, one more documented incident of you telling an unsubstantiated tale about another person in the agency, and you will be subject to suspension." During that same conference, Jackie's boss should note that dealing with the personnel problems her behavior has created takes considerable management time, which is a serious misallocation of resources.

5. Len, a stockbroker, has been capitalizing on "inside information" to make considerable profits for himself, sometimes at the expense of other brokers' clients. Although Len has not committed a documented, illegal act, his manager

can insist that Len publicly disclose such information before making personal investments. Although what constitutes *inside* information is sometimes difficult to determine, Len's manager is better off with this approach than simply encouraging him to "be more honest."

6. Herb, an office manager, is a difficult person to locate during office hours. His boss probably won't achieve good results in improving Herb's attentiveness to the job by pleading with Herb to avoid his "escapist tendencies," but he can insist on a 40 percent decrease in unexplained time away from the department.

7. José, a factory manager, refuses to settle any disputes that arise among his foremen. Instead, he refers all of these, as well as other difficult problems, to his boss. José's boss is unlikely to achieve the results he wants by encouraging José to be more confident and decisive, but he can specify what problems he feels José must handle by himself. He might also urge that José attend a decision-making seminar as a possible antidote to some aspects of his decision-making problem.

8. Ted, a state senator, lies to his constituents—behavior that is weakening his party. The party chairman may engage in some exhortations about the need for honesty in public life, but he is more likely to achieve the intended results if Ted is told that he will lose the party's backing next year unless he stops making untrue public statements.

9. Tim, an advertising and sales promotions manager, delays decisions so long that two of his subordinates and one advertising agency have resigned in the last year. His manager can work out a realistic timetable of how much time what types of decisions should require. If Tim cannot adhere to this schedule, he will be replaced. In the meantime, Tim may be encouraged by his company to attend an interpersonal development workshop to give him some additional understanding into the reasons for his procrastination.

10. Fritz, the director of research and development, has established an enviable record of patents and publications. His subordinates have complained, however, that Fritz has catapulted to fame by using their ideas and giving them too

little or no credit. His manager, who does not want to lose the creative contribution Fritz makes, must, nevertheless, confront him with his deviant behavior. Calling Fritz a plagiarist or a thief will be much less helpful than establishing a sensible review plan to insure that all contributors to a project achieve appropriate credit.

Confronting Fritz or anyone of the nine other managerial deviants just mentioned in a nonhostile manner is an important step in bringing about a behavior change in the direction of nondeviance. The stage is now set for the development of a strategic plan.

6

Developing a Strategic Plan

Deviant behavior among managerial workers can be brought under control without the wholesale dismissal of all those whose on-the-job behavior departs radically from what is considered acceptable in the current environment. What constitutes managerial deviancy must ultimately rest upon a subjective judgment of where the outer limit of tolerable behavior lies. During one phase of American military history, for example, it was considered acceptable for a general to order a private to wash the general's car, mow his lawn, and run errands for his wife. Commands of this kind, under present cultural standards, may be considered an abuse of power for personal convenience (even if still legal). A general who used his formal authority in this manner today would therefore rightfully be considered a managerial deviant.

Coping with, combating, dealing with, controlling, or eliminating managerial deviance is best accomplished with a strategic plan, a circumstance similar to the accomplishment of any worthwhile organizational objective. Unsystematic attempts to control deviance, such as a gentle reminder to a person to see his family doctor or take a well-deserved vacation or stop pushing so hard, are not necessarily incorrect; they are simply incomplete. What I am proposing is a prescription for overcoming deviant behavior that

105

has a net financial and time cost much lower than unsystematic attempts at overcoming the same problem. An often-repeated phenomenon at all levels of organizational life is that managers devote a disproportionate time to their few *problem people*. Once the assumption is accepted that deviance must be dealt with when it surfaces in organizations, it follows that effective and efficient methods of control are more desirable than ineffective and inefficient ones.

Deviance and Disease

Before going ahead with the strategic plan to combat managerial deviance, it is important to examine an underlying philosophical issue. According to the framework (philosophical point of view) used here, all forms of deviance should be considered maladaptive behavior that is basically learned. Some forms of maladaptive behavior are more maladaptive than others. The junior executive who uses the office copying machine to reproduce 12 copies of his son's cub scout roster is practicing a mild form of managerial deviancy. But if the same junior executive backdated a memo to prove that he warned his company about an impending product failure, he would be practicing a severe type of deviancy. Whether mild or severe, abusing copying machine privileges and backdating memos are both manifestations of managerial deviance.

Classifying all forms of managerial deviancy as maladaptive behavior rather than illness engenders the most controversy when behavior such as compulsive gambling, alcohol abuse, and drug dependence is considered. Alcoholism and drug dependence are classified by the American Psychiatric Association as personality disorders, which is similar to the concept of maladaptive behavior put forward here. A different point of view is taken by the many physicians who describe alcoholism as a *disease* or an illness. Marvin A. Bloc, former chairman of the American Medical Association's Committee on Alcoholism of the Council of Mental Health, states:

> Alcoholism is primarily a medical problem. As with
> every other disease, the patient should consult his phy-
> sician at the first opportunity. When a patient uses al-
> cohol as a drug to produce certain reactions rather than
> as a social beverage, he may be in the early stages of
> problem drinking or alcoholism. He should see his
> doctor.[1]

The major benefit derived from labeling alcoholism or
drug dependence as a disease is that such a classification
points to the gravity of the problem. Diseases are dysfunctional and therefore must be dealt with promptly. Two unfortunate corollaries stem from classifying alcoholism (or
any other form of managerial deviancy) as a disease. First,
the manager may feel that because the subordinate is *diseased* or severely *ill,* he can't be dealt with as a normal employee. Second, the alcoholic, drug-dependent person, compulsive gambler, or sex exploiter finds it comforting to be
classified as diseased or ill. Illnesses are still viewed by most
people as entities external to themselves that can only
change if they are treated by an external agent, such as by a
physician or medicine. Many drug addicts or alcohol abusers—managers and nonmanagers alike—have conveniently
rationalized: "I'm just not in control of myself. I want to get
better, but I'm ill. I must find a cure."

Many examples of aberrant behavior stem from disorders
of physical origin or from mental illness. As was noted in
the Preface, conditions such as organic brain syndromes,
psychoses, and neuroses fall outside the purview of our
analysis of managerial deviance. Should a senile chairman
of the board in a family-owned business occupy most of his
working hours inspecting the building for termites, he
would not be considered a managerial deviant in our classification scheme. Instead, his correct diagnostic label probably would be presenile dementia; he should be referred to a
neurologist for study.

As a final point of clarification, it should be noted that
some forms of managerial deviance do have medical complications. Perhaps they are even of physical origin. For ex-

ample, alcoholism could be precipitated by a chemical factor within the blood system, leading to a craving for alcohol. Endocrine or enzyme imbalances are two such factors. A compulsive gambler may develop an ulcer, precipitated by his poor food habits and worry in relation to gambling. His ulcer may become so discomforting that he is able to pay only surface attention to his job as a safety engineer.

The relationship between managerial deviance and physical factors can be further illustrated by the situation of a systems analyst who suffers from migraine headaches. Assuming that her headaches are caused by factors beyond her conscious control, she will experience these headaches at inopportune times. When experiencing migraine headaches she may avoid work, feigning meetings at other places or locations within the company. Her absenteeism may become excessive. Although this woman's reaction to her job or home situation (a psychological factor) may precipitate her migraine headache, it results in a physically disabling condition that can only be relieved medically. Concerned that a full disclosure of her problem will lead to her dismissal or reassignment to a less demanding job, the systems analyst continues to cover up her absences in devious ways.

Whether or not a form of managerial deviance has medical origins or complications, the manager following my system of deviance control must still play an active role in combatting deviance.

The Control Model in Overview

My strategic plan for dealing with managerial deviance is presented in Figure 6.1. Considerable reasoning went into the choice of the term *control model. Control* is an unpopular word from the point of view of the humanist and many members of the youth culture. It connotes a second party imposing his or her will on another individual, that the controller imposes standards of behavior on the person being controlled. I use this concept of control in the objective sense, as advanced by John B. Miner in his control model of human performance. "This model focuses on those cases where some deviation from an established standard occurs."[2]

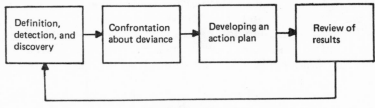

Regenerating the cycle

The Control Model for Dealing with Managerial Deviance

My control model deals with radical departures from acceptable behavior, such as the variety of forms of managerial deviance already described. New forms of deviancy are discovered almost weekly and reported to the public. An alarming example is reported by the Senate Permanent Investigations Subcommittee:

> . . . gross abuses of adolescent patients in CHAMPUS-funded [Civilian Health and Medical Program of the Uniform Services] facilities were revealed. Unaccredited "psychiatric hospitals" were paid thousands of tax dollars for "therapy" that included beatings, injecting boys with their own urine, burying them in shallow graves, chaining them in handcuffs and leg irons, and confining them in a "dungeon."[3]

For now, we will take a brief excursion through the control model for dealing with managerial deviance. Before attempting to control managerial deviance, though, we must define *deviance*. As mentioned above, *managerial deviance* is maladaptive behavior stemming from a variety of personality or value defects that results in poor job performance and/or disruptive interpersonal relationships on the job. Deviant behavior off the job is only of concern to management when its adverse consequences carry over to the job. An elaboration of the first two phases of this model has already been presented. The phases labeled *developing an action plan, review of results,* and *regenerating the cycles* are given separate treatment in later sections of this chapter.

The strategic plan for handling deviance assumes that some managerial deviants are worth salvaging. Firing is thus considered a last resort, because it reflects failure on the part of both the organization and the individual. In instances where acts of managerial deviance cross the borderline into outright criminality, firing may be necessary. Firing or suspending the deviant individual may ultimately be necessary in other forms of deviancy, but this action should be postponed until constructive attempts at behavior change have been given a reasonable chance.

Service Manager.   Jim is the manager of a branch of Automobile World. Larry, Jim's regional manager, has received numerous complaints from customers that Jim's branch has been making unnecessary repairs (a form of deviancy). There have been no complaints that Automobile World has charged for repairs not performed or that the work done was shoddy. Instead, customers contend that some of the services provided could have been postponed or not done at all. Phase I, detection and discovery, is now complete.

Larry must next confront Jim with the complaints he has received. He schedules a meeting with Jim, advising him in advance they "have some important things to talk about. Allow at least an hour." Larry's opening comment about the alleged deviant behavior is: "Jim, I have heard complaints from your customers, more complaints than we're getting from any other branch. A complaint that keeps recurring is that your shop is laying services on people that they don't need or want." After 30 minutes of heated discussion on this topic, Jim agrees to compare his repair records with some standards established by the company. Larry points out to Jim that comparisons between Jim's records and company standards need further study, but some trends are apparent. For instance, Jim's branch has sold substantially more new transmissions and complete brake jobs than any of the other branches. Perhaps more telling, his average charge per customer is considerably above average.

Jim is given the opportunity to defend his branch in the discussion. Larry points to some statistics, rather than accuse Jim of being a deviant. Labels may not be helpful in this situation. Jim argues: "Look, my customers are poorer than most of the customers in our other branches. They don't have the money to buy a new car, so they come here to get their jalopies patched back together. Then they cry like babies when they have to pay the bill."

Despite disagreement between Larry and Jim about the gravity of the charges, some specific behavioral objectives can be established in the next phase—developing an action plan. One objective is to "create business practices such that customer complaints about unnecessary repairs are reduced by 50 percent." Larry intends to use positive motivators when Jim engages in nondeviant behavior in the forthcoming weeks. For instance, when he hears no complaints for a week, he will let Jim know by phone that "you've had a good week with respect to what we talked about last week. Nobody complained about overcharges or unnecessary work."

Larry also intends to make light use of *negative motivators* if the positive ones do not bring a change quickly enough. One approach will be to send Jim a letter containing both a photocopy of the complaint letter and a reprimand whenever a letter of complaint is received. Larry and Jim also agree on a date by which complaints should be reduced to a normal level.

Phase IV, review of results, is similar to a performance review session under a management-by-objectives system. Larry and Jim will review his repair records and compare them with company standards, and then discuss Jim's feelings about the performance review. During one of these review sessions, Jim makes a comment that shows his behavior is becoming less deviant but that he still has a normal need to defend his integrity: "Okay, I've been telling my men that some of our customers are penny-wise and pound foolish. I said to hold back on repairs unless the customer's car will break down without the repair. It may cut into our bonus and hurt our morale, but I know you fellows at regional have an image to maintain."

Regenerating the cycle is the final phase, indicating that in management, control of deviant behavior is a continuous process. Larry must be prepared to detect deviant behavior (even about other practices) at any time. Should deviant behavior reappear, the cycle is reinstated. Deviance control may be inactive in any one period, but once the system has been implemented, it should not be discontinued by the organization.

Developing an Action Plan

The core of the suggested program for dealing with deviancy in a job situation lies in an action plan. *During this phase of the strategic plan, specific goals relating to constructive (nondeviant) behavior are established.* Equally important, a program is developed, designed to bring about the desired improvements. A program, or *game plan,* of this nature involves the person manifesting deviant behavior, his manager, and possibly internal staff people and outside professionals. A well-designed action plan for combatting deviance has five components.

Goal-setting is perhaps the most vital part of the action plan. Following the logic of management by objectives (or any other systematic approach to performance appraisal), improvement goals must be carefully chosen. In some instances of managerial deviance, the deviant behavior is so unacceptable that the goal or objective is self-explanatory. For example, a young CPA who appears on the premises of a client stoned on marijuana has a self-apparent objective: "Immediately reduce to zero the instances of being under the influence of marijuana during working hours. Failure to achieve this objective will result in automatic dismissal with 30 days severance pay."

Objectives established for the control of deviant behavior

must include both the type of behavior considered acceptable (for example, no borrowing from petty cash to cover personal debts) and the date by which this change must occur (in this case, the person involved might be given 30 to 40 days to clear up the quasi-legal maneuver). Ideally, the superior should be able to state the objective of ending deviant behavior by the next working day, but many forms of deviance respond better to a transition than to an abrupt change. Absenteeism or chronic tardiness are two examples of this. A manager who has been staying away from the office six days a month might be able to make the transition to two days and then one day of absence quite easily. A sudden shift to "almost perfect attendance, except for legitimate medical emergencies," will be much less likely to occur.

The participation of subordinates in setting objectives for overcoming deviant behavior on the job is fairly important. As with any other system designed to change attitudes or behavior, the involvement of the person who will do the changing is desirable. In many instances, however, if the deviant person is serious about change, he should set improvement goals without the intervention of management. In situations where the person deemed deviant expresses a sincere interest in change, mutual objective-setting between superior and subordinate becomes all the more worthwhile.

A helpful summary of the characteristics of effective goal-setting has been prepared by Stephen J. Carroll, Jr. and Henry L. Tosi, Jr., based on their research at the Black & Decker Manufacturing Company. According to their analysis:

> The first critical phase in setting objectives is the statement that describes the end state sought. This statement should be
> 1. Clear, concise, and unambiguous.
> 2. Accurate in terms of the true end state or condition sought.
> 3. Consistent with policies, procedures, and plans as they apply to the unit.

4. Within the competence of the man, or represent a reasonable learning and developmental experience for him.

5. Interesting, motivating, and/or challenging whenever possible.[4]

These characteristics can be considered an ideal toward which to strive. Deviant behavior offers more complexity in goal-setting than does the setting of "normal" work objectives. By way of illustration, I have developed a list of 10 sample objectives relating to managerial deviance. Note that all of them are specific, both to the type of behavior considered acceptable (end states) and the time by which any change specified should take place.

1. Phase out wholesale TV and jewelry sales business conducted on company premises within 30 days.

2. Reduce personal time away from office to two hours per month within 60 days.

3. Seek outside professional help for drug abuse problem within seven days.

4. Reduce instances of "bad-mouthing" your colleagues to people outside department to zero within two weeks.

5. Respond to all intra- and interoffice memos within seven days. Accomplish this increased speed of decision making within 45 days.

6. Reduce the average time of lunch break to one hour within 30 days.

7. Reduce by 80 percent the average discrepancy between date of shipment and actual shipment. Achieve this increased accuracy within 45 days.

8. Eliminate immediately all instances in which you tell the media people one thing and company employees another about the same issue.

9. Write no more than one memo per quarter that is devoted primarily to criticism of another person or department. Accomplish this by the beginning of the next quarter.

10. Withdraw from the marketplace within 30 days the pyramid sales program you have developed for our line of pocket calculators.

Establishing goals and objectives for managerial deviants must frequently include ordering the person exhibiting deviant behavior to seek outside professional help. Without relying on outside resources, the manager attempting to cope with (or change) deviant behavior places himself in the precarious position of running a private practice of psychotherapy on company time. The manager dealing with the deviant subordinate should make direct or indirect referrals. If the manager is familiar with Gamblers Anonymous, for example, the compulsive gambler might be urged to contact that organization. Another approach is for the manager to refer the managerial deviant to an intermediary. A physician affiliated with or employed by the organization, or a personnel specialist familiar with community resources might then serve as the actual source of referral to an outside agency or mental health professional.

An important distinction can be drawn between the passive referral of the deviant to a professional helper outside the organization and the approach advocated here. Following the dictates of our action plan, the manager plays an active role of expressing approval and disapproval. When progress is made by the deviant individual in using outside help, the manager expresses approval or encouragement, thus giving positive reinforcement. Similarly, disapproval (negative motivator) can be given when agreed-upon outside help is neglected. These approaches are illustrated in the following interchanges.

MANAGER: Tim, how are things going at AA?
SUBORDINATE: Pretty good. The strongest drink I've had in two weeks is Bitter Lemon on the rocks.
MANAGER: Terrific. That sounds like real progress toward beating this problem once and for all.

In contrast:

MANAGER: Mike, how are things going at AA?
SUBORDINATE: Oh, the chapter you sent me to looked
                 pretty well filled. Besides, most of the
                 people there were just two steps re-
                 moved from Skid Row. I don't think my
                 problem is that serious.
MANAGER: I think your drinking problem is very se-
                 rious. As we agreed in our discussion, if
                 you don't change your drinking habit,
                 you'll lose your job here.

An essential ingredient of our action plan for modifying
deviant behavior is the establishment of a meaningful program of positive and negative rewards, designed to encourage nondeviant behavior and simultaneously discourage deviant behavior. Chapters 7 and 8 deal at length with these
artful maneuvers, but a few preliminary comments will
suffice here. The basic reason for using a systematic program
of positive and negative motivators is that behavior has a
higher probability of being influenced in a positive direction under a systematic than an unsystematic (random) approach.

Behavior modification and its approximate synonyms for
the same phenomenon—behavior shaping, contingency
management, social learning, applied behavioral analysis,
and applied learning techniques—have been the subject of
public controversy. One factor underlying this controversy
is the exaggerated notion that all forms of behavior modification involve aversive techniques such as psychosurgery,
drug injections, and electric shock. Another misconception
is that behavior modification in organizations is simply the
generous use of pats on the back and words of encouragement.

In the action plan we are discussing here, the manager
looks for negative and positive motivators that are uncom-
plicated, unpatronizing, easy to administer, and within his

power to dispense. For instance, unless a manager owned a company it would not be within his power to give a reward of $100 whenever a *chronic procrastinator* made a prompt decision. But that same manager might say: "That quick decision you just made really hit the target dead center. You saved us $10,000." An appropriate negative motivator in a similar situation—one where a decision is delayed—might take the form of a memo saying: "Here is precisely what I was talking about. Your delay in making that decision involved an opportunity cost of about $10,000. Here are the details. . . ."

Another potential alternative in developing the action plan is *environmental change.* Many psychologists would argue that changes in behavior of any kind have a higher probability of occurring when you change the environment than when you attempt to change the person. Deviant behavior thus might be reduced by altering those circumstances in the environment that are possibly precipitating that particular form of deviancy. A field salesman who has developed alcoholism might be relegated to inside selling until his drinking problem is under control. A manager who attempts to sexually exploit subordinates might be demoted to an individual contributor position where he no longer has power to abuse. A manager who is perpetually involved in internecine battles with other departments might be placed in a managerial position where other departments are less dependent on him. Such a juxtaposition assumes that interdependency breeds conflict. For example, one company successfully interchanged the quality control and purchasing managers. The quality control manager was now in less conflict with others and the purchasing manager welcomed the rounding experience.

Environmental change in the above instance was combined with the other elements in the strategic plan. The former quality control manager attempted to be less combative in his new work relationships, and his manager periodically reviewed his progress. Working under a new pattern of interpersonal relationships, he was able to begin his program of personal development (behavior change) with a clean slate.

Modeling. In limited circumstances, modeling can be incorporated into the action plan for behavior change. According to the behaviorist concept of modeling, the learner imitates the specific skills or behaviors of a model. The manager attempting to bring about nondeviant behavior in a subordinate might find it uncomfortable to hold out himself or herself as a "model of nondeviant behavior." Nevertheless, the astute manager can point toward other key people in the organization who achieve their work and personal objectives without resorting to deviance.

One college president used modeling to help his director of athletics find an alternative to offering extralegal inducements to potential recruits for the football team. In this instance, the model used was the basketball coach from a competitor school who had a winning team, yet abided by conference regulations in recruiting athletes. A public relations specialist describes how his boss effectively used modeling as a technique for behavioral change:

> Ross really sent me on the right track about the PR function. I had started out in the business believing that you should tell the customer he is always right, no matter what a dingbat you think he really is. If a client was messing up the environment with industrial wastes, I would tell him that the government was being picky along these lines. If he had an atrocious idea for a speech, I would tell him that the idea was great, but the public just wasn't ready for it now.
>
> Ross began to talk to me about how devious I was. Instead of giving me long lunch-hour lectures on the importance of being ethical, he showed me how he operates. I'll never forget the time he took me to one of his biggest clients to tell them what they were doing wrong. They wanted him to build a story about what great community citizens they were. Ross told their president in no uncertain terms that the company had to first become good citizens of the community. After that important

first step, their efforts could be publicized. Ross showed me what to do by following him in action.

Review Sessions

Once the action plan is completed and implemented, progress toward attaining its objectives must be measured. Review sessions are the logical procedure for both discussing progress about and helping the smooth implementation of the action plan. Review sessions, at best, are essentially counseling sessions. The manager attempting to bring about behavioral change in his deviant subordinate must review performance and administer positive and negative motivators within the context of being an effective coach. A few basic principles relating to coaching and counseling subordinates deserve mention.[5]

Of prime importance, the manager counseling the subordinate must display a helpful and constructive attitude in the review sessions. (It might be argued that unless a manager possesses a friendly and helpful attitude, no review sessions will be scheduled. The person exhibiting deviant behavior would be asked to resign immediately, with no attempts at behavioral change by the manager.) An exemplary statement during the first review session would be: "How are things going in your attempts to be more factual in your discussions with subordinates [attempts to cut down on your drinking, and so forth]?" Without the expression of a helpful and constructive attitude, the person being coached is likely to perceive the review sessions as routine procedures to document his or her problems.

Listening is fundamental to the review process. Giving the person whose behavior is under review a chance to talk about his problem will sometimes hasten the process of behavioral change. Although the general orientation of this book calls for the systematic administration of positive and negative reinforcement, other approaches to modifying behavior should not be ignored. While talking about his attempts to deal with deviancy, the subordinate might arrive at some new understanding that hastens change. During a coaching session about his Machiavellian behavior, one middle manager said: "I guess one of the reasons I jockey around for position so much is that I'm not yet very confident of my true abilities."

Job problems which might be hampering the deviant person's progress should be solved. The superior should routinely inquire, "Is there anything I'm doing [or not doing] that could be interfering with your making the changes we agreed upon?" A furniture store manager was being counseled about his deceptive pricing policies, which had led customers to believe they were receiving merchandise at prices below cost. Asked if he needed any more help from his boss in getting his pricing policies straightened out, the store manager replied: "Don't blame me for what happens. You have me pulling in two different directions at once. You tell me to be more straight about pricing. Then I get a company directive saying that we have to dump so much new merchandise before the end of the year. The only way we are going to get rid of that much merchandise that quick is to come up with some pretty tricky pricing."

A similar line of questioning about job-related problems can also reveal that the action plan may require recalibrating. Modifying an action plan thus becomes an important aspect of the review sessions. Tom, an engineering manager with a penchant for making promises to other managers, which he does not keep, told his boss, Arnie: "Okay, I know I've got a problem. We've talked about it. I'm trying to change. But please stop breathing down my neck. I don't mind talking about my follow-through once and awhile, but every day is too much."

Review sessions should be held at optimal intervals. More frequent ones are required for more serious problems of deviancy. Correspondingly, less problems require fewer review sessions. Assuming that the person being coached shows a positive interest in moving away from deviant behavior, review sessions about once a week should suffice for most forms of deviancy.

Review sessions should be called any time the situation

requires them. Should a drug-abusing advertising copywriter appear stoned, it is best to conduct the review session as soon as he has returned to normal mental functioning. A widely accepted principle of good performance-appraisal practice is not to store up observations about poor performance for annual or semiannual sessions. Similarly, instances of grossly deviant behavior should be handled as close to the time of that behavior as is feasible.

Documentation of both deviant and nondeviant behavior should be part of the review sessions. This is a procedure of considerable importance. Instances of deviant and nondeviant (in a situation where deviant behavior was likely in the past) behavior should be written down as they occur for later use in a review session. Documentation can lead to meaningful confrontation. A statement such as, "You are still having a problem with staying around the office," is more likely to meet with resistance than the statement, "I needed to consult you about a problem last Thursday. I couldn't locate you, and nobody else seemed to know where you were." Documentation of positive (nondeviant) behavior can serve as a subtle form of social reinforcement. Thus a devious manager might be told: "Terry, a lot of people have mentioned to me what an open person you've been lately. What you are doing is certainly improving our interdepartmental relationships."

Regenerating the Cycle

Any system must have the capacity for regeneration. Combatting deviant behavior manifested by one individual or a group of individuals should not be considered an event that occurs only one time. Review sessions lend themselves to a regenerative process. Each review session gives the manager an opportunity to confront again the person being counseled about specific acts of managerial deviancy. Detection must precede confrontation, as is indicated in the first phase of the control model.

The phrase *regenerating the cycle* implies an important

observation about human behavior. Behavioral changes are
rarely permanent. An individual who changes in one direction may reinstate old behavior patterns under new stresses.
A staff specialist who found lying to be a convenient way of
coping with vexing business problems may, under an appropriate program of coaching, discontinue lying about job-
related issues. Under the stress of worrying about job security, that same staff specialist may again resort to lying.

Industrial Engineer. Reed, a corporate-staff, industrial
engineer, had several times been admonished about his devious tactics of obtaining information. For about a year,
Reed conducted his work in an uninspired fashion. At that
time his boss mentioned to him that he and his staff had really not come up with any major improvements for the company in quite some time. Stu, his boss, speculated that such a
large staff might not be needed for the limited problems they
had been solving lately. Concerned about job security, Reed
visited a manufacturing facility now managed by a newly
appointed plant manager. One week after that visit, Stu
called Reed into his office to talk about Reed's newly surfaced deviant behavior. Stu describes what happened:

> What Reed didn't realize was that the new plant man-
> ager, Lloyd, was craftier than he. Apparently when
> Reed visited the plant, he gave Lloyd the standard con-
> sultant's pitch: "Unless you indicate you would prefer
> it otherwise, everything you and I talk about is confi-
> dential. I'm here to help. Are you experiencing any
> problems in the organization that you would like to
> share with me?" Lloyd proceeded to tell Reed that
> his entire staff was about to jump ship because of dis-
> couragement about bringing an outsider in as plant
> manager.
> Lloyd then telephoned me, repeating the conversa-
> tion he had with Reed. Lloyd used this technique as a
> strategy to find out early in a relationship if he could
> trust a person. He would drop them some false, almost
> bizarre information and see if it leaked. Sure enough,
> Reed fell for the trap. The first day back from his field

trip, he told me he wanted to talk to me in confidence about a sensitive situation in one of our manufacturing facilities.

What About Self-Help?

Research conducted in recent years about human motivation in work organizations has repeatedly hit upon the theme that most managerial personnel are driven toward self-fulfillment on the job. Somehow the concept of self-fulfillment, or self-actualization, has been confused with questions of morality. Self-fulfillment, in the perception of many people, is morally sound; therefore people seeking self-fulfillment will do so by moral means. Furthermore, if people want self-fulfillment, they will struggle to improve their own behavior in a righteous direction.

A more realistic appraisal of the relationship between self-fulfillment and deviancy is that many people choose deviant behavior as an expedient way of accomplishing their goals. A well-documented psychological fact is that self-fulfillment is best achieved through the attainment of goals the individual thinks are important. Many forms of managerial deviancy—particularly those involving the quest for power and personal gain—are attempts to achieve self-fulfillment.

A related issue about self-help and deviancy is the question, "Why would a mature person need to be manipulated into becoming less deviant?" *Just state the problem and give that deviant person an ultimatum. Change or leave!* Changing human behavior has never been that simple. Few people can modify a long-standing pattern of managerial deviancy in response to one verbal warning.

Self-help is the most helpful in overcoming managerial deviancy when it includes a person *wanting* to manifest nondeviant behavior. Thus the alcoholic who wants to conquer his addiction, or the power abuser who wants to manage people less corruptly, has taken the first step toward behavioral change.

Finally, the intangible concept of self-help reaches its

peak of effectiveness when the deviant individual begins to find nondeviant behavior more rewarding than deviant behavior. A skillful manager, by appropriately juggling, dispensing, arranging, or manipulating positive and negative motivators, can help the formerly deviant person achieve that desirable state.

7

Rewarding Nondeviant Behavior

A manager's most effective technique for helping a deviant subordinate to behave in a less deviant manner is ready for implementation at this point in our prescription for managerial deviance. Previous steps have laid the groundwork for systematically giving positive reinforcement for nondeviant behavior. No new company-wide program of deviance control need be installed; no new department need be created; no elaborate behavioral science technology need be learned by the superior involved.

What is required in this phase of our system is that the manager attempting to encourage nondeviant behavior make an effort to demonstrate by action precisely what kind of behavior the organization approves of. In our strategic plan, positive motivators are given preference for the control of deviant behavior because of their demonstrated superiority over negative motivators in changing behavior. All positive and negative motivators discussed are those kind of reinforcers most managers have at their disposal. Although of theoretical value, it would be fatuous to suggest that a manager provide a subordinate with a 10 percent salary increase whenever he behaved in a nondeviant manner in a significant situation. Equally fatuous would be the recommendation that a manager periodically administer mild electric shocks to any subordinate who continues to exhibit deviant behavior after the initial confrontation session about such behavior.

Readers familiar with the technology of behavior modification may at this point wonder why I am recommending a seemingly incomplete system of changing the behavior of deviant managers.[1] There have been reports in the popular media about elaborate systems for shaping the behavior of juvenile delinquents in geographically isolated settings. Similarly, patients in the back wards of hospitals have been helped to relate more constructively to the world through the technology of behaviorism. Several reasons underly my hesitation in recommending such an elaborate system.

Work organizations, as they are presently constituted, will not allow an elaborate system for modifying deviant behavior. Managers would require much more power over resources than they currently have or probably ever will have. Few managers, for instance, would be able to alter the benefits package a subordinate receives, no matter how deviant his or her behavior. Few managers could get the cooperation of more than a few other organizational members to help him modify the behavior of one other person. Another important reason for my position is that behavior modification has not yet been field-tested on a large-scale basis with resourceful, intelligent, generally well-functioning, albeit deviant, people. Behavioral science has moved in the right direction, but it still offers guidelines rather than a definitive technology for making human beings more responsible in their actions. In essence, I am suggesting that nondeviant behavior can be encouraged, and deviant behavior discouraged, by the manager involved, acting as an experienced coach armed with a mixture of psychologically sound information and common sense.

Choosing the Appropriate Reward

Motivating other people to do anything involves finding an incentive that appeals to them. All theoretical positions about work motivation support this basic premise. In attempting to reward nondeviant behavior, the manager must thus find a relatively potent reward for the deviant person (one that "turns him on"). In addition, that reward, or incentive (terms that can be used interchangably), must be at the manager's disposal. The person dispensing the reward, or holding it out as an incentive to be received when nondeviant behavior is displayed, must have the authority or skill to use the reward. Keith, a field service manager, gives an example of a manager who lacked the skill to use praise as a reward or incentive:

> Ben should never have taken a job managing people. He was brilliant, well organized, and a firstrate administrator. But he was no leader. He simply didn't know how to compliment a person for a job well done. The best example I can think of is when our group had reduced overdue service calls by 85 percent. Customer complaints about poor service had therefore been dramatically reduced. Our objective had been to reduce overdue service calls by 50 percent. When I had my review session with Ben, his opening remark was, "I note that you have exceeded your customer service objective by 35 percent. Let us now focus on areas where your department must make some additional improvements."

After a manager has analyzed which incentives are available to him in dealing with subordinates (the list of rewards presented later in this chapter includes the majority of rewards available in most organizations), an attempt can be made to match rewards with individual preferences. One important clue is to observe what kind of reward the individual under consideration tends to talk about. Some people, for instance, talk about receiving recognition for their efforts, while others focus on receiving more money or status. In some instances people who exhibit deviant behavior on the job are concerned about job security ("There is no chance I will lose my job for this one incident, is there?"). A potent reward to administer to such an individual after he has behaved in a manner deemed appropriate by the manager might be: "Tom, I see you handled that shipping delay problem in a very straightforward way. That's just what we talked about in our session last week. Keep that up and you'll be around here a long time."

Another individual might reveal by an occasional comment that he or she can be motivated by comradeship. Some people satisfy many of their social needs in job situations. Having lunch with the boss is a meaningful incentive to them. An effective reward for nondeviant behavior in this situation might be: "Gloria, I note that you've had no problems with any department heads for a long time. Let's have lunch today so you can fill me in on what's happening."

When past behavior hasn't provided a clue to an individual's most appropriate incentive, experimentation is necessary. Beginning with the obvious rewards (such as praise and other kinds of verbal recognition), several can be tried until one or two seem to click. As one manager said in a management development conference: "It took me a year to learn that Sam would rise to peak performance if I only gave him feedback every day on how well he was doing."

A possible moral dilemma facing the manager attempting to reward nondeviant behavior is that deviant individuals are rewarded for simply being nondeviant, while nondeviant individuals must be exceptional or adequate to receive rewards. The distinction to be drawn between rewarding nondeviant behavior versus adequate or superior job behavior lies in both the *magnitude* and *type* of reward. An appropriate reward for six months of refraining from deviant behavior might be a cost-of-living adjustment in salary. Superior job performance during that same six-months period might command a 12 percent salary increase. To illustrate further, simple feedback on performance might be an appropriate reward for a managerial drug abuser trying to rehabilitate himself while an appropriate reward for superior performance might be promotion to a more challenging assignment.

Find Some Constructive Behavior to Reinforce

Evoking actual changes in the behavior of a subordinate begins with the process of reinforcing any behavior that moves in the desired direction. However elementary this process sounds, *shaping* of behavior toward a planned-for objective increases the probability that larger-scale changes will be forthcoming. An analogy to athletics will help illustrate this principle. Assume that a tennis coach is working with a young woman learning to serve. Virtually her entire service at this point deviates from acceptable (effective) practice. An important device her coach can use to change (shape) her behavior in the direction of a more effective service is to reinforce anything she does that approximates the correct physical movements. For instance, on the advice of her coach, the woman might drop her racket back behind her shoulder. At this point a "behavior mod"-oriented coach would say, "Good news, Marcia. I see that you are dropping your racket back the right way." Marcia has taken the first step toward hitting a nondeviant serve.

Market Forecaster. Randy, a staff assistant involved in market forecasting, illustrates how the principle of "find some behavior to reinforce" might work in a business setting. Randy was perceived by his boss (and a psychological consultant working with the company) as a devious individual. High on the list was his habit of interpreting facts in the direction he felt management wanted to hear, rather than making a more objective interpretation. For instance, when asked by management to give them an up-to-date forecast of intermediate-range demand for a particular product, Randy would try to determine what answers they were hoping to hear. To obtain such information, he once asked the marketing vice-president's secretary: "What kind of mood is Irv in these days? Does he seem optimistic or pessimistic about business? Do you think he wants to expand or cut back on marketing operations?"

A developmental objective for Randy was to become more professional and detached in his presentation of information to management. He was given the assignment of predicting demand for a proposed product—a semipermanent tentlike structure designed to keep outside workmen warm and dry while installing pipes or digging house foundations. Randy recognized that he would not have been asked to predict the demand for this product if somebody in management didn't believe in its marketability, so in his report, he painted a glowing picture of the need for such a product. However, he dampened the overall optimistic predictions with a sombre statement that "some people would predict a 10-year depression in the construction business due to a possible long-term shortage of mortgage money." Randy's manager felt that his report did not go far enough in gauging the impact of the construction business economy on new-product developments in that field. Nevertheless, the report was not entirely devious. In a review session with Randy, his boss commented: "Your construction tent report showed some signs of objectivity. That's real progress and the kind of thing I want to see more of."

Purchasing Manager. Giving positive reinforcement to any behavior, however elementary, pointed in the direction of nondeviant behavior often brings about a chain reaction of improvement. Bill, a former alcoholic purchasing manager, describes one aspect of his recovery process:

> I finally began to grab hold of myself about a year ago. My manager knew I had a drinking problem. I had tried in the past to conquer it, but always slipped back into the same trap of drinking one too many when I became tense. I swore off drinking one weekend. I walked into the office Monday morning at nine sharp with a freshly pressed suit and a suntan. My boss said: "Bill, it's nice to see you here so early and looking so alert." I felt terrific and took exactly 45 minutes for lunch. Being complimented for coming to work on time doesn't seem like something a mature person should require, but it was a big boost and step forward for me.

Scheduling of Rewards

Another essential element in rewarding nondeviant behavior is the proper scheduling of rewards.[2] Rewarding a person for moving in the direction of nondeviancy involves the dual consideration of (a) how frequently to give positive reinforcement and (b) how close in time rewards should follow the appropriate behavior. Many instances of failure to accomplish agreed-upon objectives are related to neglect of these considerations.

Years of experimentation with behavior modification with a variety of subjects in laboratories (rats, pigeons, and people, among other living organisms) and in live organizational settings suggests that people should be rewarded often but not every time. This is fortunate for managers with busy jobs; it would be impractical to reward a subordinate every time he or she exhibited nondeviant behavior in a situation where deviant behavior might have been exhibited in the past. I place emphasis on the latter point because even the most managerial deviant is not deviant in *every* situation. Rewards must be tied to situations where deviant behavior frequently manifested itself in the past.

A bank officer had established a conflict of interest situation between his employer and a personal finance company. He would refer people who were refused loans by his bank to the finance company on a commission basis. (He, of course, helped make the decision about turning people down for loans at his bank.) Assuming (a) he is not fired by the bank and (b) that the bank will work with him toward becoming less deviant, the reinforcement he receives should relate to his disposition of poor credit risks. Should the proportion of people judged to be acceptable risks (consistent with bank policy) increase while his mysterious referrals to that particular finance company decrease to zero, he might receive some form of positive reinforcement. However, all his other nondeviant, unexceptional job behaviors need not be singled out for reward.

A disadvantage of rewarding every nondeviant behavior by an individual is that the person might become dependent on reinforcement to exhibit normal behavior. A plumbing and heating contractor decided to send notes of appreciation to slow-paying customers when their bills were paid promptly. When he stopped this practice, several of his customers slipped back into their delinquent (deviant) payment schedules. Asked why this had happened, one customer said: "The letters stopped, so I figured prompt payment wasn't important any more."

The ideal frequency of reinforcement is the one that works the most effectively. A practical strategy is to begin programming a schedule of reinforcements by rewarding (for example, with verbal praise) nondeviant behavior whenever it appears and gradually diminishing the frequency to an occasional reward. Some people require more reinforcement than others—even for activities that can rightfully be *classified as normal expectations of the position*. As one executive secretary commented: "I'm well paid and well treated. But I expect something more in the way of appreciation than a once-a-year, cost-of-living salary increase."

One problem in implementing a program of behavior modification in a work environment is that of providing a reward in close time proximity to the behavior that requires reinforcing. In a laboratory experiment, the experimenter is immediately at hand to reward correct behavior, whereas managers often are not physically present close to the time in which the nondeviant behavior occurs. Ingenuity is sometimes required to tie reinforcement to the desired behavior. The president of a printing company had been working with one of his sales representatives to get him to give customers a more honest estimated date of delivery. In visiting a large customer, the president was asked why he just received from the president's salesman a longer than usual estimated date of delivery. That afternoon the president sent a telegram to the salesman, stating in part: "Congratulations. Bryant Company angry now but will respect us better in long run. Honesty wins in our business."

Although few managers attempting to help a particular subordinate become less deviant can tie rewards in close time proximity to the manifestation of nondeviant behavior, one helpful commonsense principle can be followed: reward the desired behavior at the earliest feasible opportunity. Often this earliest opportunity will be three minutes before next week's staff conference (verbal rewards are very economical with respect to time) or at an informal lunch five days after the event. If they are to be of maximum value, rewards for nondeviant behavior should not be delayed until the next scheduled review session.

A Panoply of Rewards

Although the amount of authority most managers have for dispensing positive reinforcers to subordinates is limited, the number of rewards that can be used to motivate subordinates is greater than many managers realize. My purpose in describing the rewards below is to relate them to the modification of deviant behavior, rather than to give an overview of the complex subject of work motivation. Astute observers of organizational life will be able to expand this list. My list of rewards is intended to be comprehensive but not exhaustive. Several of the rewards may appear similar to each other, which presents no real problem in their application. A confounding factor, however, is that some factors are positive reinforcers for some people but negative reinforcers for others. Providing one manager an opportunity to attend a staff meeting because he has been less deviant lately, might be reinforcing for him, while another manager might regard attending that same staff meeting as punishment.

Feedback on behavior is a potent, economical reward available to almost every manager. The simple process of informing a formerly deviant person how he or she is doing in behaving less deviantly (particularly if progress is being made) is reinforcing. Review sessions, if properly conducted, are thus motivational. Giving a person no information about how they are doing in overcoming deviancy can be discouraging and therefore demotivational. Even when a person has an accurate self-assessment of his progress, external assessment is helpful. Informal, casual types of feedback are frequently effective. One manager suddenly moved in the direction of becoming a less deceptive person when his manager told him, "The feedback I'm getting lately is that your credibility index has gone way up."

Praise, encouragement, and related types of evaluative reinforcers[3] are also readily available and economical. The

now retired director of management training for a multibil-
lion-dollar organization once commented to me: "Doesn't
the field of psychology or management have anything else to
offer besides telling us in 135 different ways how to be nice
to people?" Although this executive had a limited understanding of the applications of behavioral science in management, he did recognize the intrinsic motivational value
of saying positive things to people. Most people (masochists
excluded) have an almost genetically based desire for encouragement, to be liked. This need persists from infant-
hood until death.

Many managers would argue that a person should not be
praised or given approval for not being deviant. Such actions would be tantamount to storeowners sending thank-
you notes to those who pay their bills on time, or police persons giving out tickets of appreciation to those who obey
speed laws. But conventional thinking may have to be revamped if the spreading problem of managerial deviance is
to be effectively handled.

Approval, essentially another evaluative reinforcer,
should be expressed openly to achieve maximum value as a
reward. Receiving approval for one's actions is highly reinforcing to most people. It also implicitly indicates what kind
of behavior is condoned by the organization. In behavioristic terms *condoning* something means giving positive reinforcement to a particular act of behavior. Telling another
person that his behavior meets organizational requirements
is a direct way of expressing approval. A pharmacy manager
had been, in effect, boosting prices by not giving company-
authorized discounts to senior citizens unless they requested the discount. His manager confronted him about
this deviant behavior. Later when the number of senior citi-
zen discounts increased by 30 percent, his boss told him: "I
like the effort you've made in granting discounts to senior
citizens. This is the anti-inflationary and humane direction
we want our business to take."

Recognition is another almost universal reward, or incentive. Wide ranges of people will display motivated behavior
(increase their expenditure of effort toward goal attainment)

if they believe that some form of worthwhile recognition will be forthcoming. Recognition can be used as a reward for nondeviant behavior or promised to a person if nondeviant behavior persists. Although more research is needed along these lines, giving recognition for behavior already exhibited has some superiority over the promise of recognition for behavior yet to be exhibited.

Vance became a champion of equal opportunity for blacks despite many years as a value deviant in this area. For many years Vance had systematically excluded blacks from supervisory and staff-level jobs in his plant. His president had several sessions with Vance, discussing the need for overcoming his antiblack prejudice, at least in the job environment. A month later Vance promoted two blacks to supervisory jobs and hired a black manufacturing engineer. A local newspaper reporter preparing a feature story about blacks in the labor force inquired at Vance's plant. As the situation developed, a photograph of Vance shaking hands with one of the black supervisors appeared in the newspaper. Vance received enough positive reinforcement in the form of recognition to radically change his core attitude toward hiring blacks for supervisory and staff positions.

Comradeship can be a potent incentive if used genuinely. The companionship of colleagues forthcoming from working in most organizations is one reason why many people persist in working for them. Being close to other people during working hours is reinforcing. Deviant managers also find companionship or comradeship a worthwhile benefit to be derived from the work environment. For some people, comradeship from a superior is even more rewarding than companionship from peers, because the former is mixed with approval from a person with formal authority.

Assuming that a manager has an honest liking for a deviant subordinate, he can offer comradeship as a reward for exhibiting nondeviant behavior. Margot, for example, might be seen as a managerial deviant by her boss because of her approach to winning political battles. According to her boss, Dorothy, when Margot and she are in dispute over an issue, Margot takes her case to Dorothy's boss, a male. Margot uses

her charm and allure to win her point. Dorothy confronts
Margot about this mildly deviant behavior. Later, as Margot
becomes less deviant in her approach to settling interpersonal disputes, Dorothy befriends her. Luncheon conferences and social invitations are two ways of offering comradeship as a reward for desired behavior. As with any other
reward or incentive discussed here, it may not work for everybody and it may not work all the time, even though it is a
generally effective reward.

Job security is generally used as a negative, rather than
positive, reinforcer. In essence, maladaptive personnel are
told to adapt to organizational requirements or leave *(shape
up or ship out).* The promise of job security can work as a
strong incentive for an individual who feels that he is becoming less desirable on the job market because of his maladaptive behavior. A blatant appeal to a person's need for job
security can be an effective motivator.

Dan, the head of the business department at a small
university, was conducting his job in a deviant manner. In
order to free up time for speaking engagements and consulting, Dan gave a clerk in his department almost total responsibility for assessing the prior academic record of incoming
students. Complaints by students and a routine audit revealed such gross errors as giving some people credit for
flunked courses and not giving people credit for equivalent
courses with different titles. Dan's boss, Vincent, was able to
successfully change Dan's deviant behavior pattern by an
appeal to his need for job security. His motivational discussion with Dan focused on the fact that Dan would be eli-
gible for tenure the next academic year. "But I cannot recommend you for tenure unless you do a better job of evaluat-
ing students' prior records."

People who dislike or distrust systematic methods of motivating people would label the foregoing and similar inci-
dents as *bribes.* My objection to the term *bribe* is that it is
evaluative rather than descriptive. All forms of motivation
through external rewards (cash bonuses, good grades, con-
tests, and stock options, to name a few) must then also be
called bribes. Under ideal circumstances, internal motiva-

tors can be used to overcome deviant behavior (motivate
people in general), but few people are motivated solely by
internal motivators. The topic of internal motivators and
managerial deviancy will be reintroduced in the last section
of this chapter.

Money is more readily used as a negative than as a positive reinforcer in attempting to modify deviant job behavior. Only when the person under review clearly understands
that additional money will be forthcoming for exhibiting
constructive behavior can money (usually in the form of a
salary increase) be seen as a positive incentive. Money can
be used as a reward for exhibiting nondeviant behavior over
a prolonged period of time. Thus: "John, it looks like you
have conquered your problem of making false promises to
customers. I can now rightfully recommend you for a salary
increase." In most circumstances money is used as a negative motivator in relation to deviant behavior. A person
comes to recognize that being deviant has resulted in a
suspension of salary increments or bonuses. Something of
positive value (money) is being taken away (punishment)
because of maladaptive behavior.

A favorable performance appraisal is a logical and practical reward for nondeviant behavior. Under most performance-appraisal systems, the individual being appraised
hears and sees the results. Calling a previously deviant individual an "outstanding performer" (when it is true) would
have a high impact toward changing behavior. A troubled
individual may also perceive an average rating on a performance appraisal as having positive reinforcing properties.
Receiving an improved rating—perhaps from below average
to average or above average—is also a positive reinforcer for
the person who formerly exhibited maladaptive behavior.
Performance-appraisal ratings are symbolic reinforcers
because they represent other reinforcers such as approval,
acceptance, and even money. In sum, favorable performance-appraisal ratings are a potent reward for exhibiting
nondeviant behavior.

Confidential information is a subtle, yet sometimes effective positive reinforcer. As a person manifests more non-

138   *MANAGERIAL DEVIANCE*

deviant behavior, he or she can be provided with more confidential information. In complex organizations, receiving inside information has come to develop reinforcing properties. People like to be *in on things,* and the receiving of confidential information places them in that situation. Sharing confidential information with a subordinate is reinforcing also because it communicates trust and confidence in that person—a form of approval or acceptance.

Dispensing confidential information has high motivational properties in working with people whose deviant behavior takes the form of deviousness. Assuming that a manager is willing to take risks, as the person becomes less devious, he or she can be shown more trust. A statement of high reward value in this regard would be: "Linda, we've had no more reports of your leaking information to people who don't have a need to know. I feel I can trust you more now, so here is some sensitive information I would like to share with you."

Challenging work assignments are perhaps the most potent motivators an organization can offer an individual. Since challenging work assignments are not in unlimited supply, they cannot be freely dispensed. People whose behavior has never been maladaptive are waiting in line for such assignments. With these limitations in mind, rewarding a person's movement toward nondeviant behavior with a choice assignment can still be accomplished. Particularly effective is the practice of giving a person a special assignment in the area of their deviance. For instance, a plant manager who was slipshod in his attention to safety practices in the past might be placed on a corporate safety committee as a reward for his giving recent attention to safety.

In one company a former drug addict works in the personnel department as a specialist in dealing with drug-abuse problems of employees. His management showed faith in his attempts at rehabilitation and offered him a challenging assignment that served as a reward for his nondeviant behavior. Simultaneously, the company benefited from a knowledgeable person in a sensitive assignment. Many nonprofessional drug counselors in community settings are former drug users themselves. For obvious reasons, they are better able to establish rapport with their clients than are professional workers with no history of drug abuse.

Promotion has more reinforcing properties than most other rewards administered in organizations because of the continued emphasis in our society of equating upward mobility with success. Promotion can be used as a reward for having discontinued deviant behavior or as a promised reward for not exhibiting deviant behavior in the future. For instance, a division general manager might be told that he would be seriously considered for a promotion to a larger division if he would develop a better record of providing career opportunities for culturally disadvantaged people. In instances where the deviant behavior involves personal habits (for instance, alcoholism), promotion as a reward for being nondeviant might be interpreted by other organization members as an undeserved reward.

In general, only when a person's maladaptive behavior pattern is well circumscribed (for example, polluting the environment or discriminating against minorities) can promotion be used as an incentive. Even in this situation the deviant individual would have to be an outstanding performer in other aspects of his job. Maladaptive behavior patterns involving personal habits such as alcohol abuse often result in a wide variety of administrative and technical errors. A careful analysis of a person's job performance might reveal that he has established too poor a record to be rewarded with a promotion in the foreseeable future.

Improved working conditions represent a meaningful reward to people who are laboring under poor working conditions. The deviant individual under review who begins to exhibit nondeviant behavior can thus be rewarded with better clerical support, a private office, a company car, or the services of another person to answer his telephone. Providing a person with additional comforts is another direct way of expressing approval of that person. The latter adds to the reinforcing properties of improved working conditions. As one territory representative said: "I knew darn well that I was on probation with the company because of a few strange deals I had made with customers. I straightened out and they began to make life easier for me. They trusted me enough to give me an additional allowance for hiring part-time secretarial help. It made me feel that I was again part of the company. For awhile I felt like I was some sort of a leper left to rot."

Stimulating coworkers is a form of reward not widely used in organizations, yet it has highly reinforcing properties. Brighter, more capable people tend to be reinforced by working with other brighter, capable people. As an individual moves away from deviant behavior and toward constructive job behavior, he might be given the chance to work with a more select group of individuals. A transfer to a department staffed by intellectually stimulating people, or a temporary task-force type of assignment are two examples.

Marty, a hostile cost accountant working in a factory cost-estimating department, was counseled by his boss about his hostile relationships with shop floor people. Marty's basic retort was: "Okay, I'll be nicer to people, but I don't think I belong in this type of operation. I get along much better with professional accountants than I do with shop people." After six months of "being nice to people," Marty was rewarded with a transfer to a financial analyst position on the corporate staff—a position he finds more rewarding. Parenthetically, this is an example of changing the environment rather than changing the person, in order to bring about changes in personal behavior.

Improving a person's chances to succeed is a novel, yet to be widely practiced, form of positive reinforcement. Psychologists Ted Gupton and Michael D. LeBow have reported some exploratory research in this area, which can serve as a starting point for further investigation.[4] In their study, two part-time telephone solicitors were required to sell new appliance service contracts and renew old ones. Since renewal contract calls and sales were easier to come by than new contract calls and sales, "the opportunity to sell five renewal contracts was made contingent upon one new service contract sale." Results were encouraging, in that "the percentage of sales for both types of contract increased when the contingency was in effect and decreased when this contingency was removed."

Application of this concept to deviancy management involves giving the formerly deviant individual an improved opportunity to succeed as he exhibits constructive behavior. For instance, an otherwise capable production supervisor might have a pattern of not reporting minor accidents in order to improve the safety record of his department (and therefore, his performance appraisal rating). As his safety reports appeared to reflect a higher degree of honesty, he might gradually be given the chance to add employees to his department with a better safety record or be assigned to supervise a more inherently safe production operation. Thus his chance for establishing an improved safety record (and therefore succeeding in an important aspect of his job) would be *contingent upon* his showing nondeviant behavior (providing honest safety reports).

Status symbols must be included in any contemporary discussion of potential reinforcers used in modifying the behavior of people. Although research has indicated that status symbols are not effective motivators for most people, status has motivational value for others. Special privileges given to members of management often derive their reinforcing properties from the fact that they are essentially status symbols. Such things as private parking spaces, membership in the executive physical fitness program, and executive dining room privileges offer comfort and convenience, but their primary motivational value appears to be derived from their value as status symbols.

Status symbols are usually tied closely to considerations of rank. Membership in an executive physical fitness club, for example, is usually restricted by rank in the organization. A manager attempting to reward nondeviant behavior by manipulation of status symbols must generally resort to less grandiose symbols. Repainting a manager's office because he has behaved less deviantly is one such reward for the status-conscious deviant. Another more easily administered symbol is to invite the now less deviant manager to lunch with another executive of high rank. One manager was chastised for cheating on his business mileage allowance—a mild form of managerial deviance. When he established a six-months record of not repeating this behavior, he was rewarded with an air-conditioned car. Driving an air-conditioned car may be a trivial benefit to many people, but it *can* serve as a reward for having overcome deviant behavior.

Nondeviant behavior itself should be the ultimate reward to the managerial deviant. A widely misunderstood aspect of behavior modification is that it allows no room for a person to be intrigued by work itself, that people are prodded along only because of their quest for external rewards. The ideal circumstance under any system of behavior management is to have the task itself become reinforcing. To illustrate, a nicotine addict may use external rewards to help him overcome cigarette-smoking. He might put one dollar in a piggy bank for every day he doesn't smoke. He might receive praise from his wife and children for not smoking. He might find clean ashtrays and unburned clothing as reinforcing. Ultimately, not smoking itself will develop reinforcing properties. Enjoying the freedom to enjoy food without combining it with a "nicotine fix," being able to sign a contract without lighting a cigarette, being able to sit through a movie without squirming for lack of a cigarette will combine to making nonsmoking reinforcing within itself.

Similarly, the managerial deviant who engages in excessive political battles with other people may come to enjoy relating to others in a more constructive, less devious, manner. The fruit farmer who pays fruit pickers livable wages and provides them with acceptable living conditions may eventually find running a morally sound operation rewarding. The landlord who increases profits by shutting off heat from two until five in the morning (thus contributing to much discomfort and some illnesses) may find treating tenants humanely to be a rewarding experience. Once pointed in the right direction by astute management, many formerly deviant managers may discover that nondeviant behavior is self-rewarding.

8

Discouraging Deviant Behavior

Despite its unpleasant connotations, punishment cannot be dismissed as an important strategy for the control of aberrant behavior, providing it is used in combination with the reward of nondeviant behavior. Encouraging, or rewarding, nondeviant behavior should generally precede the discouraging, or punishing, of deviant behavior. Punishment is of two general types. Withdrawal of a positive or satisfying situation (for example, taking away a manager's company car or private secretary) is one type. A second is the imposition of a penalty (for example, fining a baseball player who punched an umpire or fining an executive who purchased stock on the basis of inside information). Punishment can be used directly, or it can be reserved as a contingency if behavior does not change.

What's Wrong With Punishment?

Civilizations would be almost devoid of crime and other forms of wrongdoing if punishment or the threat of it were a competely effective way to change behavior. Most countries have outlawed crime and specified penalties for criminal behavior, yet crime continues at a persistent, if not accelerat-

143

ing, rate. Administering severe punishment to children seems to encourage rather than discourage subsequent criminal behavior. Juvenile delinquents are typically raised in family situations where physical punishment is the favored disciplinary method of both mothers and fathers.[1] Business organizations that impose the heaviest penalties for the infraction of work rules are the least likely to have harmonious union-management relationships. In the world outside, as well as inside work organizations, punishment has its disadvantages.

First of all, punishment leads to high anxiety, which may interfere with job effectiveness. A manager with a drinking problem who is placed on probation may become so tense that his need for alcohol increases. Asked how he felt about being placed on probation by his company, a manager said: "It's a weird, spooky feeling. I wasn't bad enough to be fired, but I'm not good enough to really keep. I'm not really out of the company, but I'm not really part of it either. It makes me very tense."

Middle Manager. Punishment frequently leads to counterhostility, expressed directly or indirectly. Because of the deeply ingrained taboo about a manager physically striking another, few managerial deviants will strike their boss when punished, yet counterhostility may express itself in other ways. Barry, a middle manager with considerable talent and promise, kept irregular office hours. Management decided to punish him by transferring him laterally to a position in Cleveland—a situation he did not welcome. Barry explains his counterhostile maneuver:

> I got even with "corporate" on a grand scale. My wife and the children hated the idea of moving out of the New York area to Cleveland. But once we got there, we found it wasn't half bad. It seemed much less crazy than putting up with the harassments of New York. We found a home in a Cleveland suburb for $15,000 less than our home in New Jersey. This gave me a nice lump sum for investment. Ten months after the company had moved me, including paying the total relocation costs,

plus a small cash relocation allowance, I quit the company. Two of our customers and I set up a solid little business. If the company hadn't zapped me by sending me to Cleveland, all these good things wouldn't have happened.

Corporate Recruiter. Withdrawal and alienation are also not infrequent responses to being punished. Instead of feeling closer to the organization, the managerial deviant subject to punishment or the threat of punishment may find it more difficult to identify with organizational goals. Jay, a corporate recruiter, explains the circumstances surrounding his loss of enthusiasm for his job:

At the outset let me state that I was guilty of some pretty stupid financial tricks. I wound up on the verge of bankruptcy because I got hooked on the traveling man's Achilles' heel—spending the credit card company's money on personal bills. Once started, it's hard to get off the cycle. We were in a period of heavy recruiting activity, which meant I was traveling about 15 days a month. I was using my credit cards for everything, including air travel. It wasn't unusual for me to have a monthly travel expense of $1,200.

Once, by accident, I submitted my travel voucher promptly and received payment within a week. When I received the check for about $750, it dawned on me that the various credit card companies wouldn't be sending me their bills for another two weeks. I used the "loan" to buy a color TV. It didn't take long before my monthly bills were about 125 percent of my monthly income. Then came additional loans to cover old loans.

When creditors approached my company, they responded by taking away my expense account privileges. To do this effectively, I was placed in an almost clerical job within the department. I no longer cared about the company. All I cared about was my predicament. Finally, when I was in better financial shape, I quit the company to take a job with an employment agency.

Perhaps the most serious drawback to punishment (particularly when it is severe) is that the punished behavior is temporarily suppressed rather than eliminated. Criminal behavior usually resurfaces, if not intensifies, when an incarcerated person returns to the outside world.[2] Recidivism rates of about 80 percent are not unusual. Punishment typically leads to suppression of a behavior pattern rather than its extinction, because new ways of behaving are not taught in the punishment process. A conflict deviant might be punished for his constant fighting with other organization members. This punishment (perhaps a demotion) might be more effective (lead to positive changes in behavior) if the punished individual were given an opportunity to learn how to accomplish things through people in nonconflictual ways.

What's Right with Punishment?

Assuming that punishment is carefully combined with some encouragement or reward for behaving in a nondeviant manner, punishment may have some useful consequences to the organization and the individual. Additionally, punishment works best in organizations when it is administered impersonally.

Punishing people for deviant behavior is an example of the type of actions that will not be tolerated in the organization. Assume that a top executive promotes a relative from the position of mail room attendant to administrative assistant at three times the pay, after one year of service. The organization might punish the executive by asking him to make a public apology about the spurious promotion and decrease his relative's salary 50 percent. Other organizational members will see a clear example: that blatant violations of the merit system will not be tolerated in the organization. Models work best when they are drawn from the top of the organization.

A subtle advantage of punishment for the individual deviant is that it might help him cope better with guilt feelings. The theory that people want to be punished for their transgressions because of guilt pangs associated with not being caught may have some merit. To the extent that an individual expects punishment for deviant behavior, punishment may have some psychological value to that person. Extending this analysis one step further, some executives seek chastisement from the public as a way of being punished for past wrongdoings.

Recently the governor of a large state gave his personal secretary a new title and raised her salary to $44,310 per year. Working as a special assistant to the governor, she is paid more than many state agency heads. Her duties include overseeing assorted details of the governor's office and screening his appointments. She may be of more value to the governor than most agency heads, but that isn't the point. Receiving that salary with that job title is almost inviting a public investigation.

Punishment can be useful to the organization because it fits a popular conception of justice: deviant behavior requires retribution. Morale in small work units tends to be lowered when a blatantly deviant individual goes unpunished or even unnoticed by management. Correspondingly, morale within the work unit is temporarily elevated when a deviant person receives an appropriate punishment. When top management transferred and demoted the sex exploiter of subordinates referred to in Chapter 1, people within his department were relieved. A typical sentiment expressed by a work group member was: "I wish they had stopped him sooner."

Punishment has a therapeutic shock value for some people. The shock of being severely punished for deviant actions gives them an emotional understanding of the real implications of their behavior—an understanding that could only be intellectual without actual punishment. Several managers have commented to me that one of the kindest acts they have done for an alcoholic subordinate was fire him. Often expressed is the sentiment, "An alcoholic has to hit rock bottom in order to begin the climb back up toward a normal life."

Another example of the shock of punishment having

therapeutic value involves a college football coach caught encouraging his players to take amphetamines before a game. Expelled from the conference, he now works at a smaller college. His attitude is: "I'm kind of glad I got my knuckles rapped. I now keep college sports in proper perspective. Winning is important, but not at the expense of potentially ruining the lives of my players."

Administering Punishment

According to our strategic plan for dealing with aberrant behavior, punishment should be used after attempts have been made to encourage nondeviant behavior through the appropriate application of rewards. In many instances, confrontation alone will bring about the desired change in behavior. From that point on, review sessions can be used to reinforce and encourage continued nondeviant behavior. When all objectives are met, neither further counseling nor administering punishment is necessary. One such curtain-closing statement might be: "It looks like we're getting no more complaints from customers about unwarranted charges. Why don't we drop the issue unless the problem comes up again?"

Which punishment to select is a difficult decision. In some cultures in the past, punishment was designed to fit the crime. A pickpocket might expect to have his hand cut off or a voyeur to be blinded. In selecting a punishment from among the group of specific punishments described below, it is best to begin with the mildest form of punishment that might be effective. For instance, just the process of offering criticism or providing feedback about deviant acts may be sufficient discouragement to decrease the probability that deviant behavior will reappear. Negative feedback or criticism might take the form of a memo or a phone call. For example, after a staff meeting in which a marketing manager gave an elaborate rationalization of why this quarter's sales objectives could not be met, his boss might call him or send him a memo, saying: "Les, I noticed a lot of blame-passing on your part today. You pointed the finger at everybody but the people in marketing for your failure to make projections this quarter."

Punishments should be used in order of increasing severity (while at the same time rewarding significant nondeviant behavior). Following the above example, when verbal reprimands don't work, a more potent form of punishment might be tried. Sometimes the promise of a more severe punishment may be effective. "Les, if you continue to criticize others and don't take a critical look at the problems in your own department, I may have to reassess whether you belong in this job."

In Chapter 7 I mentioned that rewards for nondeviant behavior should be administered intermittently. However mild the punishment for deviant behavior, it should be administered whenever the deviant behavior appears. Acts of managerial deviancy should never go unmentioned whenever they're recognized.

The late Douglas McGregor gave some suggestions about disciplining people in work organizations, which has some application toward punishing deviant behavior. According to the red-hot-stove rule, discipline should be analogous to touching a very hot stove. "When you touch a hot stove your discipline is immediate, with warning, consistent, and impersonal."[3] Assume that Herb, a systems analyst, has been telling various people in the organization that he has the power to ask that they be fired if they do not cooperate with him in his studies. His manager learns of this deviant behavior and confronts Herb, stating that such behavior will not be tolerated (*immediate*). Herb realized when he took this position as systems analyst that the position involved limited formal power. Herb knew he would have to *ask* for the cooperation of people, not use implied authority (thus he received *warning*). He has been treated *consistently* with others in the organization. Any other systems analyst who abused power would be similarly advised of his or her unacceptable behavior. *Impersonality* is generally difficult to convey when administering punishment, but Herb's boss makes an effort in that direction. He criticizes Herb's behavior rather than attacking his character. For example, the statement, "Herb, you're a devious person without conscience," would have been taken quite personally.

A Selection of Negative Motivators

As with positive motivators (rewards), negative motivators can be used by either presenting the negative condition directly or by threatening to impose the motivators. The imposition of a penalty after an act of deviance tends to be more potent than the promise of a penalty if another act of deviancy is committed. Whether an actual penalty is imposed or only threatened, it must be emphasized that negative motivators should be used only in conjunction with positive motivators. If a person is to be penalized for deviant behavior, he must also receive some kind of reward for manifesting nondeviant behavior.

Aversive punishment of a physical nature, such as electric shock, beatings, and the injection of harmful substances into the bloodstream, are omitted from the list because they have no place in work organizations. In addition, they are deviant acts themselves when administered to unsuspecting people. Electric shock might be considered moral and nondeviant when used in a laboratory. Subjects in such experiments are voluntary and are aware that the noxious stimulus to be used as a punishment *is* electric shock.

Feedback on maladaptive behavior is an efficient and effective negative motivator. The simple process of telling a person that he has exhibited deviant behavior can be an effective, mild punishment for many people. Feedback is essentially a reconfrontation. For example, a manager might be confronted with the observation that he lies to people about work-related matters. Later, should new instances of his lying be uncovered, his manager might provide new feedback on this behavior (another confrontation).

Managers sometimes feel uncomfortable about revealing the source of second-person feedback about deviant behavior. Pat, a partner in a management consulting firm, used a phrase to open a feedback session about maladaptive behavior that neatly glossed over the issue of the source of the information. A consultant working for him had been accused of using unethical tactics to gain advantage in a client situation. In an attempt to gain the cooperation of middle managers in a client organization, he would casually say: "I've just come from the president's office. He thinks it would be a good idea if you and I got together to talk about problems." A middle manager who knew Pat (the deviant's consultant's boss) phoned him to tell him of the consultant's attempt to gain an advantage.

Later that week Pat called the younger consultant into his office. His opening line in reference to negative feedback was: "Word has gotten back to me that you've been manipulating people again." The phrase *word has gotten back to me* avoids the side issue of the identity of the informer and gets directly at the central issue of maladaptive behavior.

Criticism is another readily available penalty that requires no formal program or administrative approval for its use. Criticism goes one step beyond negative feedback about maladaptive behavior. In addition to citing the undesirable behavior, a negative comment is made about that behavior and/or the person involved in that behavior. As described in the earlier discussion about confrontation, criticism is more likely to bring about changes in behavior when the act rather than the person is criticized.

Whether the deviant act or the deviant person is criticized, criticism usually hurts. It is therefore a potent penalty and has the potential disadvantages of most forms of punishment. The defensiveness and anxiety associated with criticism often manifest themselves in the criticized person's physical appearance. One production manager described how his plant superintendent reacts to criticism: "I think Joe would take more kindly to a punch in the stomach than personal criticism. When I criticized him for using company trucks to help him with his Christmas tree business, his face first turned white, then it turned red. Then he almost cried. Next his mouth got so dry he could hardly talk. At the same time he would cup his chin with his hand in a gesture that looked like he saw a UFO land on his front lawn."

Criticism is sometimes ineffective as a negative motivator

for the opposite reasons of those just mentioned. Some people become so defensive when criticism is levied against
them that they deny its existence. Criticism is thus heard but
not emotionally accepted. Many an errant individual who is
finally asked to leave an organization denies ever having
been criticized for poor performance. Closer examination of
some of these situations reveals that the person simply did
not pay attention to the criticism.

Withdrawal of privileges is a negative motivator more
widely used in prisons and homes for juvenile delinquents
than in executive suites. One important logistical disadvantage is that privileges are usually assigned according to rank
in an organization. Thus every manager at or beyond a certain grade level is automatically placed on the executive bonus compensation plan. Should that executive be accused of
abusing power in his relationships with a small supplier
(such as forcing the supplier to provide goods or services at
an unacceptable profit level), he could usually be denied
only executive compensation if he were lowered in rank.
Similarly, that same executive might have rights to a company car because of his rank. His immediate manager (unless
that person is the company owner) would most likely require a special ruling to have his company car privileges
suspended or cancelled.

It would be equally awkward to impose penalties such as
withdrawing a manager's right not to punch a time card or
eat in the executive dining room. Withdrawing such privileges tends to drive a person away rather than closer to his
organization. When a person's bond of identification with
the organization begins to weaken, it is not unlikely that his
job motivation will also begin to suffer. In rare situations it
is necessary to withdraw privileges because the particular
form of deviancy is related to the abuse of that privilege. For
instance, an executive might have his country club privileges withdrawn or suspended because he has been playing
an unreasonable amount of golf on company time!

Documentation of deviant behavior works as a penalty of
more than average impact. Documentation usually takes the
form of making an official entry in an individual's perma-

nent record, such as a personnel file. People at all organizational levels dislike having negative comments about their personal behavior become part of their permanent record. In some organizations entries made in an employee's personnel record, beyond routine information, tend to contain negative information. Thus one personnel manager commented: "I can tell if a person is going to be difficult to transfer by the thickness of his personnel jacket. The real troublemakers who have been with us for a long period of time have records an inch thick."

In addition to making supplementary entries in one's personnel file, a manager can permanently record deviant behavior in the appropriate place on a performance appraisal form. Whatever the format, the documentation of deviant behavior presents a vexing problem to the deviant person. As long as he stays with that organization, people have access to negative information about his character.

In addition, negative information about that person might be passed along to the next organization that considers hiring him. As one rehabilitated alcoholic told his boss: "I'm happy that you gave me the chance to pull myself together. I'm willing to stay with the company and make a new record for myself, providing one condition is met. I want every bad thing said about me removed from my permanent record." Few organizations are willing to launder a person's file; while few individuals want to remain in an organization that has them permanently labeled *maladaptive.*

Punishing a person via documentation has the potential of creating a difficult management problem. Many states grant people the legal right to examine their personnel files. Should the person you consider deviant take strong exception to your documented statements about him, he might find a lawyer to champion his cause. Unsupported statements about a person's character (particularly, written statements) could constitute the subject matter of a libel suit. For instance, a statement such as "Larry is a pathological liar" entered on a performance-appraisal form could eventually cost its author (or the company involved) a considerable sum of money. Much less libelous is the statement, "Larry's frequent incorrect statements to people create much confusion in the department." Any boss has the right to cite errors in a subordinate's job performance.

Probation has a long history as a form of punishment for wrongdoing in organizations at the production-worker level. The individual who transgresses is told: "One more wrong action and you will be fired." Probation, more than most other forms of negative motivation, pushes a person toward loosening his or her emotional bonds with the organization. A logical alternative to probation is to set a target date for overcoming a particular form of deviancy, with the ultimatum that dismissal will be the consequence of the persistence of deviant behavior. Placing a person on probation adds very little to the effectiveness of punishment.

Aside from giving a person the feeling that he is virtually out of the organization, probation is an unsophisticated form of punishment. It gives a person the impression that he is immature in addition to being deviant. A headwaiter in a resort hotel was placed on probation for having demanded kickbacks from his waiters and waitresses. One comment he made was: "Let me take my punishment like a man. If the owners don't like the way I do business, that's their prerogative. But don't treat me like I'm a little boy who has played hooky from school."

Suspension has long been used in the control of deviant behavior in the field of athletics, both professional and amateur. The deviant athletic director who violates recruiting rules may find his teams suspended from participation in conference championship competition for a year. Athletes whose physical assaults on the opposition take the form of actual fighting are often given short suspensions. People involved in managerial work are more difficult to suspend. For example, it would be awkward to suspend a deviant manager, appoint a replacement, and then reappoint him after the term of the suspension. Professional people who exhibit deviant behavior such as malpractice may have their licenses temporarily suspended. Suspension in this situation is easier to administer from the standpoint of the punisher. However, the person suspended may feel compelled to change the nature of his work (perhaps from private practice to institutional work) rather than establish a new practice.

A feasible solution to the use of suspension in complex organizations is to reassign the suspended person to another job upon his or her return. A humane president of a clothing manufacturing company suspended one of his salesman for giving rebates to customers. After his period of suspension, the salesman was given a territory in a different city. His comment to the president was: "I was wrong. I accept the punishment, and I'm grateful to start with a clean slate."

Fining a deviant manager or staff person may lie outside the province of his boss unless the manager levying the fine is the company owner. A fine has the classic disadvantage of most forms of punishment: it engenders resentment, yet does not point the way toward more constructive behavior. It smacks of retribution, thus frequently forcing the fined individual to withdraw from forming any closer identification with the goals of the organization.

On the positive side, fines are a dramatic form of punishment because of the high symbolic and actual value placed on money in many cultures. Fining groups of managers for collective acts of deviancy (for instance, neglecting safety standards or polluting the environment) is usually considered just practice by people outside the organization. Fines are also economical—they bring money back into the organization—even if they do not recapture the true cost of the deviant's actions. Another advantage of fines is that they can be perceived as impersonal, providing other people have been fined similar amounts for similar acts of deviancy in the past. For example, a company might establish a standard $200 fine for anybody caught taking merchandise off company premises without authorization. Fine systems, however, are difficult to enforce in most business firms and educational and governmental organizations. Red tape alone would discourage gaining permission to impose a fine.

Assignment to an undesirable task or job is a subtle form of organizational punishment.[4] An unfavorable assignment is usually administered for milder, rather than more severe, acts of managerial deviancy. An executive in a well-known company was once so punished.

> I'm at the top of my company now, but I had some rough spots on the way up. I began as a field salesman and received a few rapid promotions. They brought me into corporate for a big jump in responsibility. While at corporate, I was considered talented but obnoxious. I asked too many embarrassing questions and made too many waves. Finally I was sent back into the field to run one of our worst branches. I figured, if Corporate Siberia was the name of the game, I would go along with it. I learned my lesson. I did a fantastic job in our worst branch. When I was promoted back into a key spot, I became more tactful. I hope I didn't sacrifice my principles, but I became a much easier person to live with.

Demotion can be a useful punishment for certain types of deviant behavior. When a person needs rehabilitation, including a rebuilding of self-confidence, demotion to a less demanding job can be beneficial. One germane example is that of Dennis, a chief engineer who developed alcoholism. It appeared to Dennis and his manager that his drinking problem only began to manifest itself when Dennis became an administrator. In response to increased job pressures, he became less controlled in his drinking habits. Reassigned to a senior engineering position, he was able to again control his drinking. Asked about his future plans, Dennis replied:

> Right now it feels good to be the master of my own emotions. I'm doing an effective job as an engineer on some technically sophisticated work. Why spoil a good thing? When I feel that I'm in complete control of my drinking problem and that I can handle administrative pressures, I may look around for a manager's assignment. Until then, I'm happy to be doing creative and constructive work.

Firing is the next most severe punishment an organization can administer to anybody. Even more severe is giving someone a negative reference when a prospective employer makes an inquiry. As mentioned earlier, because of its shock value, firing an individual can be an effective form of behavioral change. Confronted in such a dramatic way with the implications of his own behavior, the individual may begin a process of constructive change. Until fired, that person may not have experienced a true emotional understanding of the potential negative impact on his life. Firing also gives a subtle advantage to the organization. It serves as an effective warning system for those remaining in the organization.

Firing an individual for deviancy represents a multiple failure. The managerial deviant has failed to adapt to organizational requirements. He has been insensitive to what kind of behavior is tolerable within the organization (or has found deviant behavior more rewarding than nondeviant behavior in that particular organization). Equally significant, the organization has failed in its mission of deviance control. Deviant behavior in its germinal state went unnoticed or ignored, and unconfronted. Yet another failure is that whatever talent or ability the individual in question had left to contribute to the organization went unsalvaged.

9

Inadvertent Rewards

Certain actions taken by an organization can unwittingly perpetuate managerial deviance. Drawing an analogy from parent-child relationships, parents sometimes unintentionally reward bed-wetting on the part of young children. When a child wets his bed, this action frequently elicits a predictable response from the mother or father. The child is picked up, caressed, given fresh clothing, talked to by a parent at a time in which contact with a parent is usually limited and, finally, tucked back into bed. Bed-wetting has thus evoked an entire series of actions the child finds pleasant (reinforcing). Inadvertently the parent has rewarded a pattern of behavior (bed-wetting) that he or she would prefer to discourage.

Unintentionally rewarding deviant behavior is not a widespread practice, but a high-impact, infrequent phenomenon that is difficult to identify unless a manager is sensitized to the possibility of its existence. Unfortunately, it is sometimes the managers who are trying the most diligently to combat aberrant behavior that are trapped into giving such behavior positive reinforcement.

Excessive Attention to Deviancy

Deviant behavior, exhibited by both managerial personnel and children, is sometimes essentially an attempt to gain

159

attention. To illustrate, an alcoholic warehouse manager might drink heavily because he craves the attention that his drunken behavior elicits from other people. His manager, the personnel manager, the company physician, perhaps even his family doctor, and his wife all involve themselves in his maladaptive actions. Finding no effective way of distinguishing himself by his managerial talent, the manager in question resorts to alcoholism as a way of receiving the attention he craves.

Consulting psychologist Anthony W. Martin, one panel member analyzing the "Case of the Alcoholic Absentee" for the *Harvard Business Review*, illuminates this process. Joe Parker, the alcoholic manager in question, had a ready explanation for his every disappearance from work, but generally these explanations were flimsy rationalizations. Dr. Martin comments that the company was actually contributing to Parker's immature behavior:

> Parker has been rather poorly handled at ABC Electronics Company. In not dealing firmly and explicitly with his attendance lapses and dubious excuses, the company has contributed to his lack of consistent performance. It has unwittingly encouraged him to persist in an immature maneuver which has become, over time, self-defeating to the individual and harmful to the company at a vulnerable stage in its development![1]

As a manager receives increasing attention for his deviant behavior, the deviant behavior may increase, rather than decrease, as the company would desire. Excessive counseling with a managerial deviant may have the same effect. When a manager spends inordinate amounts of time with a person who is displaying deviant behavior, that maladaptive behavior may be perpetuated. Assume that Scott has a gambling addiction that has dysfunctional consequences for both his job and family life. His manager, Phil, being sympathetic and "people-oriented," devotes a couple of hours a week listening to Scott talk about his addiction. Scott realizes, perhaps unconsciously, that terminating his addiction will simultaneously bring about a termination of conferences with his alter-therapist, Phil. Scott craves attention as much as he craves the excitement associated with gambling. He is placed in a conflict situation. He recognizes that gambling has both positive and negative consequences for him. On the negative side, gambling is threatening his job security and the stability of his home life. On the positive side, his gambling brings him both excitement (from the gambling itself) and attention from his boss (the special conferences with Phil).

Phil can help reduce the reinforcement Scott is receiving from his gambling habit by (a) reducing the thrill Phil receives from gambling, or (b) reducing the amount of attention he receives because of his gambling. Only the latter course of action is directly under Phil's control.

Mental health workers also fall prey to giving inadvertent reinforcement to maladaptive behavior. Floyd Ruch and Philip G. Zimbardo comment on this phenomenon in relation to delusions and other psychotic behavior. Their analysis is presented here because an almost identical process takes place when management overattends to the actions of an aberrant organizational member.

> It is standard procedure in many mental hospitals for the staff to ask patients frequently how they are feeling. This may focus the patient's attention on his emotional state and provide the expectation that the "appropriate" behavior is to be thinking and talking about one's feelings, unusual symptoms, hallucinations, and so on. In fact, the more bizarre the symptoms and verbalizations, the more attention may be shown by the staff in their efforts to understand the "dynamics" of the case. One patient, asked by an interviewer if there was "anything else that was bothering him," responded: "You mean *halicinations* or *sublimitions*?"[2]

Creation of Shelf-Sitters

No organization has a formal policy of rewarding managerial deviance with a promotion, yet some organizations—at least as perceived by organizational members—are guilty of such malpractice of management. In rare instances the old cliché, "He was booted upstairs," accurately describes the disposition of a particular deviant manager. It appears that promoting a person as a reward for deviance is more frequently practiced in private than in public corporations. However, this statement should not be taken as an indictment of family-owned businesses. Public corporations also may have their share of managerial deviants sitting on comfortable shelves created for their benefit.

Hardware Executive.   A disgruntled systems analyst describes the situation of Winfred, an executive in a privately held hardware wholesaler:

> Win used to be the vice-president of sales. I guess he did a pretty good job for a number of years. His forte was personal relationships. He was well known in the trade and spent much of his time building personal relationships with key manufacturers and customers. He never cared much for the thinking man's side of management—budgeting, planning, and the like. Win felt that all there was to management was to work with and through people. He prided himself on the fact that he had many friends in the business and no enemies that he was aware of.
>
> Win used to combine his favorite pastime, yachting, with his work. At first he would take customers out only on weekends. Soon he was finding excuses to entertain customers on his yacht on weekdays. He would take longer and longer weekends, claiming that he did much of his paperwork on the yacht. During the few months he put his boat away, he would still visit the yachting club during working hours. His relationship-building may have been good for business, but Win was becoming something of a joke around the office. Besides, it was difficult for members of the sales department to get an answer on a decision when they needed it. Win's absenteeism was hurting morale and probably had a negative effect on business.
>
> The president and other people on the management

team began to realize that Win's situation had gotten out of hand. John (the president) promoted our western regional manager to vice-president of sales, and a new position was created for Win. He was given the elegant title of "senior vice-president, planning and development." An office was newly decorated for him, fit for the president of a 100-million-dollar company. Win was out of the office much more than in the past. Now he could almost never be found. Win had become vice-president in charge of nothing at full pay and benefits.

However rare the elevation of managerial deviants into corporate staff positions has become, when it does occur, it fosters (rewards) deviant behavior at lower levels in the organization. Promoting rather than demoting a maladaptive manager is thus another method of unintentionally rewarding managerial deviance. Other people in the organization come to recognize that an organizational climate conducive to deviance has been established.

Deviant Models at the Top

A more general case of inadvertently rewarding deviant behavior is retaining people in key positions who manifest deviant management practices. This serves as a model for deviant behavior at lower levels. Personnel at lower levels consciously or preconsciously reason: "I, too, can be deviant if this is what top management is really like." In addition, the process of not taking action against deviance amounts to subtle reinforcement.

Not receiving punishment for an act that is ordinarily punished is a peculiar variety of *negative* reinforcement. The relief of anticipated pain (being penalized for a transgression) not being forthcoming is rewarding. Similarly the person who speeds along the thruway at 90 miles an hour and is never penalized comes to regard that lack of a penalty as a type of reward. Escaping an anticipated penalty is a comfortable feeling. To give a final illustration, the person who cheats on his income tax return tends to feel some discomfort for about a year. By that time it is apparent that no audit will be forthcoming. The relief of anticipated punishment (an audit and possible fine with interest) serves as a reward and increases the probability that cheating will be repeated on next year's tax form.

In recent years several examples of quasi-legal, deviant behavior by top management members of well-known public corporations have been exposed by the press. Cases such as these are germane here because members of top management were rewarding each other for deviant behavior. During the very time in which the most devious of these acts were perpetuated, many of the executives involved received salary increases and cash bonuses. When the deviant behavior of top management was publicly exposed (always by agencies external to the organization) it served as an indication to other organizational members that deviant behavior is actually sanctioned by the organization. As one low-ranking member of an organization so publicly exposed commented in an interview:

"Are you kidding? Of course there's a lot of hanky panky going on down at our level. Some of us are taking days off with pay to go fishing. One guy I know is buying some merchandise wholesale himself and selling it right out of our stands. If the kingpins around here pay themselves fat salaries to cheat on us and the public, then we can do the same on a smaller scale." The source of this statement works for an organization faced with the following list of fraud charges:

The former chairman disguised the firm's financial difficulties for a two-year period.

A former financial executive for the company not only assisted in misrepresenting the company's operations, but also personally profited from illegal insider stock trading. He sold over 10,000 shares of stock when he knew his company was in trouble, but the public was not yet informed. In addition, this executive and a few associates were charged with misappropriating several million dollars in corporate funds.

The prestigious public accounting firm representing the company was accused of filing false financial statements for the company.

A brokerage firm that underwrote a new issue for the firm did not inform potential customers of the true financial condition of the company.

Bonanzas for Deviants

"I can't believe it. Pete was given early retirement and a year's separation allowance. Now he has enough of a nest egg to do whatever he wants. Why should an alcoholic be subsidized by the company? Anybody who watched Pete's work habits felt he should have been asked to leave the company a year ago. Now he finally leaves on some kind of a trumped-up medical discharge. If he had a heart attack or a stroke, his separation allowance would be understandable. If Pete had lost his mind, what the company did would have been more palatable. Pete, in effect, was given a large cash bonus for being a noncontributor."

The essence of these comments were made by a disgruntled systems and procedure manager, an individual with a personal commitment to organizational efficiency. Generous separation allowances for managerial deviants serve as an inadvertent reward for deviance. Deviant behavior has been rewarded on a grand scale that is visible to many other members of management. A comparable situation occurs when an executive makes a substantial profit on the basis of stock trading with inside information. In some instances the executive is asked to leave the organization or take a cash penalty. In either case, the economic rewards forthcoming from his deviant behavior are substantial. Crime or deviancy that pays tends to be imitated by other organizational members.

Suppression of Ethical Protest

Few individuals within corporations (or other forms of organizational life) have the courage or inclination to publicly protest the wrongdoings of top management. When those rare instances of public protest lead to the demise of that individual in that organization, a predictable phenomenon transpires. The protest of managerial deviance is punished, thereby subtly rewarding deviant behavior. Punishing nondeviant behavior is tantamount to rewarding deviant behavior. Organizational members participating in deviant behavior feel reassured (experience reinforcement) when those attempting to combat deviance are suppressed.

Common sense and anecdotal evidence suggest that upbraiding top management for deviant behavior is a hazardous procedure. Albert Z. Carr, in analyzing the long-range advantages of socially concerned actions on the part of businessmen, notes:

> Perhaps there are some executives who are so strongly positioned that they can afford to urge their managements to accept a reduced rate of return on investment for the sake of society of which they are a part. But for the large majority of corporate employees who want to keep their jobs and win their superiors' approbation, to propose such a thing would be inviting oneself to the corporate guillotine.[3]

Women in industry, in increasing numbers, are filing complaints of antifemale discrimination to agencies such as the Equal Employment Opportunity Commission. Women who take such action against managerial deviancy of this nature do so with an element of personal risk (even though reprimands for filing complaints are illegal). A female manager explains how this form of suppression works:

> Filing such a complaint is much more likely to benefit some woman in the future than yourself. Of course, nobody is stupid enough to tell you outright that from now on you are a persona non grata, but you will be in trouble. What happened to me was obvious. After I filed my complaint about our company not having enough women in management, the situation improved for women other than me. I was transferred to an office

manager position that had no advancement possibilities. Two other women in the company bypassed me for good jobs within the next year. You can never prove such charges because qualifications for manager's jobs are very difficult to pin down.

In short, when top management retaliates against those who choose ethical and proper means for protesting any form of managerial deviance, a climate of acceptance for deviance is fostered. Inadvertently (or perhaps in some instances, advertently) managerial deviance is rewarded.

10

The Productive Deviant

Managerial deviants are sometimes productive people. From the standpoint of their employers, some deviant managers make a worthwhile contribution. In other instances, deviant managers who are not making a real contribution to the organization are nevertheless perceived by their superiors as productive. The phenomenon of the productive—and pseudo-productive—deviant lead many members of top management to proclaim (in reference to managerial deviance): "We have no such problem around here. Every manager in this company is making an important contribution to the corporate effort. We wouldn't have it any other way. We wouldn't tolerate that kind of thing and our stockholders wouldn't stand for it either."

The intention of this chapter is to provide some preliminary insight into one of the most perplexing facets of managerial deviancy. Deviant behavior often goes undetected for an unfortunately long period of time because the deviant manager is directly or indirectly—through his or her subordinates—making a positive net contribution to organization welfare. Managerial deviancy is frequently a subtle pattern of behavior with a gradually experienced pernicious impact. Deviancy can be a slowly festering phenomenon in a work organization.

Deviancy Can Work in the Short Run

> *Manufacturing Executive.* You college professors
> and economists tell us one of the real reasons we have
> inflation in the United States is because the work force
> is so damn unproductive. Maybe it's true that there is
> widespread inefficiency in industry. Maybe we should
> tighten up across the board and stop trying to rehabili-
> tate disadvantaged people on company time. It used to
> be that the church had the responsibility of reclaiming
> lost souls. Now industry, particularly in their manufac-
> turing plants, is supposed to rehabilitate people who
> don't know how to work and who don't want to work.
> Our company is through trying to make useful em-
> ployees out of disadvantaged minority groups who have
> no respect for work. Our hard core unemployed training
> program led to nothing but confusion in our company.
> Our older workers were annoyed because they felt that
> young blacks and Puerto Ricans were being given spe-
> cial privileges. Our production efficiency dropped
> severely once we began to job train minorities on com-
> pany time. When we found a legitimate excuse to ter-
> minate people who won't adjust to work, our productiv-
> ity rose again. My personal suggestion to the company
> has been to automate or subcontract whenever possible,
> rather than try to keep unemployables on the payroll.

Although the manufacturing executive making these statements may be morally deviant, his strategy for organizational efficiency may be valid—at least in the short run. If a gradually increasing number of people in the United States are
excluded from manufacturing employment, the long-range
consequences will be burgeoning public assistance roles
and a smaller base of potential consumers. An unwilling-
ness to attempt a *fair share* of job training culturally disadvantaged minorities is essentially a form of moral deviance.
Yet, as a short-range strategy, it leads to a strengthening of
the organization. Efficiency, and in some instances the morale of older workers, would be elevated if hard core unem-

ployed training programs and the like were abandoned.

Restaurant Proprietor. A managerial deviant from the service industry—a restaurant proprietor—took over the management of a successful gourmet restaurant. After purchasing the restaurant from the estate of its deceased owner, the new owner found devious ways to increase profits. He ordered a cutback in the kitchen staff, substituting a line of gourmet frozen foods for many of the entrées previously prepared on the premises. Profits increased dramatically. Within a year the dilution of quality in food served by the restaurant had its impact on customer acceptance. Within two years the owner closed the restaurant and opened a fast-food franchise restaurant in its place. The location proved inappropriate for a fast-food restaurant; volume was too low to yield a profit. A parking lot now stands in its place. Short-range economies, thus, were the starting point of a series of employee dislocations and customer inconveniences.

Deviancy Requires Imagination

A notable fact about many varieties of managerial deviants is that they are intelligent, imaginative people. Intelligence and imagination are fundamental requirements for expediting some of the more intricate forms of managerial deviancy. The intellectual requirements for some forms of deviancy exceed those required for comparable forms of criminal behavior. Swindles that lie within legal limits—those that are not quite blatant forms of embezzlement or fraud—are usually the product of creative intellects. When the sublegal deviant is engaged in nondeviant behavior (few managerial deviants are deviant in every aspect of their work), he is likely to be a resourceful manager. One executive who was providing ideas to a competitor on a consulting capacity was a highly regarded engineering manager. Although he had personally profited from his deviant maneuvers, he had also contributed several highly successful product innovations to his company.

Pyramid sales plans have recently acquired illegal status,

but many settlements are made out of court, suggesting that
all such plans are not blatantly illegal, assuredly punish-
able, acts. However, they unequivocally classify as examples of entrepreneurial deviancy. Called by *Time* a billion-
dollar industry and the nation's number-one consumer
fraud, pyramid sales plans illustrate the depths of imagination frequently displayed by managerial deviants.[1]

Pyramiding is a marketing technique based on multiple
layers of "distributorships." Recruits for the scheme are
gathered by optimistic letters, telephone calls, and phony
pollsters. All are invited to a revival-type "opportunity"
meeting—usually in a first-class hotel or motor hotel. "There
they are whipped into hopeful enthusiasm by spielers, who
talk about incomes of up to $108,000 a year for peddling the
company's products and recruiting new distributors."[2]

In rare instances, participants in the pyramid marketing
plans reap adequate returns on their investment. Usually
they wind up losing sums of money they can ill afford to
lose. Many who buy into such schemes have low incomes
and are looking for instant wealth. Cash set aside for retirement, weddings, or formal education is used for the pyramid
investment. The products—usually cosmetics, soaps, vita-
mins, or personal development courses taught by nonprofes-
sionals—are generally overpriced and sell poorly. A salesman must usually pay the firm several thousand dollars and
pay for "leadership training" courses in order to advance to
the position of a distributor.

Once the salesman becomes a distributor, he receives cash
bonuses for signing up other salesmen and distributors. Extra bonuses are forthcoming for any distributors whom his
distributors sign up—the pyramid effect. A basic flaw in this
scheme is that a given geographic area quickly becomes
saturated with the product and distributorships. Only a limited number of people are a real potential market for these
products or services. As a student of mine commented,
"Once Elmer took to selling_____, all his friends began to avoid him. He became some kind of a convert to the
gunk, and expected to convert all of his friends. If that gunk

did all for a car it was supposed to, the transmission and motor replacement business would be dead."

Psychopathic Personalities Are Smooth Operators

Psychopathic personalities (called *character disorders* or *psychopaths* until the American Psychiatric Association revamped their diagnostic categories less than a decade ago) include a number of entrepreneurs and executives among their ranks. With their well-developed capacity to influence other people, psychopathic personalities can be effective in many aspects of managerial work. They are particularly adept at exploiting others and projecting blame for their own socially disapproved behavior. Robert F. Pearse, in his study of "managerial hustling," has identified the subtype called the *ingratiating opportunist*, another manifestation of psychopathic behavior. According to Pearse:

> Commentators on the personality characteristics of political figures caught in . . . national political scandals describe them as anxious to please their superiors but at the same time covertly self-centered in advancing their own career opportunities. Ingratiation is a trait often pleasing to older superiors who enjoy having smooth young subordinates catering to their wishes. When ingratiation is combined with a modicum of technical competence, plus the right social connections, the ingratiating-opportunist type of hustler often has a meteoric rise in organizational life.[3]

In the process of serving their own ends, psychopathic executives often make a contribution to the organization. Part of this contribution stems from their ability to enlist the cooperation of many people in getting a task accomplished. Executives considered "promoters" or "hustlers" by their colleagues and superiors are often borderline psychopaths intent on forwarding their own career whether or not other people are hurt and resources are misallocated in their quest for success.

Marketing Executive. Neil, a marketing executive, fits the psychopathic personality category, as described by a personnel specialist:

> Neil had an emperor complex. He wanted to be big, strong, and powerful even if it didn't do the company a darn bit of good. During the boom of the mid 1960s Neil got the rest of top management on an expansion kick. He wanted to set up 75 new branches of our temporary help employment agencies. He had an elaborate set of charts, graphs, facts, and figures assembled. As you might expect, the controller threw up some cautionary signals. He kept warning Neil and his followers that not all growth is progress. But Neil pushed ahead in his convincing manner. He convinced other members of the management team that to oppose growth was an act of disloyalty.
>
> Neil set up an organizational plan calling for the creation of an executive vice-president position. Briggs, our president, believed strongly in Neil and appointed him to that exalted position. By the time the dust had settled, our firm had 35 new branches, with Neil as executive vice-president and acting vice-president of marketing. We obtained a lot of our money for expansion through an attractive sounding stock offering.
>
> Even though our industry generally does pretty well in a recession because it becomes economical to hire help only when needed, the business downturn of the early 1970s almost put our company under. Branch managers were on a commission basis. As business wasn't forthcoming, they pulled out pretty fast. Their replacements didn't understand the business. Last I heard, half of the branches closed down. Neil left for a real estate deal in the Southwest. But now the company is moving forward again, with the remaining branches doing just fine. Neil's plans were in the right direction. If he hadn't been such a glutton, he would not have

been asked to leave the company. He actually woke the company up to the need for growth.

Loyalists and Sympathizers

Managerial deviants endowed with competent subordinates sometimes achieve their objectives (remain productive) despite the fact that they themselves contribute little to the organization. By cleverly obtaining the loyalty and sympathy of subordinates, they are able to accomplish tasks required of them by their superiors. In a large organization with many layers of management, a given manager might be able to delegate almost all his measurable tasks to subordinates. When information is finally requested of him by his superior, he can rely on information supplied to him by his subordinates. Industrial psychologist Robert Hershey explains how an emotionally insecure (and possibly deviant) manager can appear productive even though he has considerable difficulty in making all but the most routine decisions: "He calls his staff together, obtains a range of decision options, presents them to his superior as his own and is complimented for the depth of his analysis."[4]

Executive secretaries have the well-deserved reputation of remaining loyal to their bosses even when it appears that the boss is no longer competent to hold office. Loyalty of this nature manifests itself in several ways. One common maneuver is for an executive secretary to parry the inquiries of others trying to contact her boss. Among the more noncommittal (and not untrue) excuses used by executive secretaries to explain a boss's whereabouts are:

"He's out of the office now and will not return until later."

"He's expected back shortly. May I leave a message as to who called?"

"He has a meeting scheduled downtown right after lunch. It could take several hours."

"His appointment calendar seems full for the next several days. Might we call you if there is a change?"

Secretarial Takeover. Executive secretaries also protect

managerial deviants (particularly alcoholics and procras-
tinators) by taking over many of the tasks expected of them
by the organization. Not uncommonly, an executive secretary might prepare a department budget or write a critical
memo for her boss (all the while being paid as a secretary
rather than an administrative assistant). Gradually the executive secretary is accomplishing much more work than
her boss, yet the boss appears productive to the organization.

In less frequent instances, executive secretaries keep their
deviant bosses productive by providing them the emotional
support they need to cope with job stresses. Laura describes
a relationship she had with a former boss:

> I worked for Ralph for close to two years. I'm glad to
> learn that he finally went for therapy and is doing much
> better now. Ralph was the most insecure manager I ever
> worked for. My secretarial and administrative skills
> were the least important part of my job. Ralph needed a
> constant ego boost and that assignment kind of landed
> in my lap.
>
> How do I know that Ralph was insecure? I could give
> you 50 examples. He was so afraid of not pleasing man-
> agement. He would fawn all over a top executive. If he
> prepared a report for an executive, he was prepared to
> rewrite it if the most minute aspect was not to that ex-
> ecutive's liking. Ralph was a nail-biter. If he had an im-
> portant meeting coming up, he would chew his nails
> about down to his cuticles. Ralph would listen atten-
> tively in the halls to find out if anybody was mentioning
> his name. If somebody said something positive his day
> was made. If he heard a negative comment, he would be
> even more tense than usual.
>
> I think I spent about two hours a day listening to
> Ralph worry out loud about things. He seemed to need
> me to say that he was doing fine, or one of his projects
> was going to make a big hit with management. He never
> asked me just to type a letter. He would also want to
> know my reaction to it. His favorite question was,

"What will management think of this?" I don't want to sound immodest, but without me bolstering his ego on a daily basis, I don't think Ralph could have held onto his job.

The Weekend Deviant

Competent, resourceful, and productive managerial personnel are sometimes deviant during nonworking hours. They deserve the label *productive deviant* because their deviant behavior patterns appear to have no spillover onto their primary job responsibilities. Mike, Leslie, and John exemplify productive deviants.

Mike, a computer scientist, is a weekend hippie. Every Friday night he dons his hippie attire and retreats to his girl-friend's apartment to become part of the drug culture. A good share of his weekend is spent "tripping" on either soft or hard drugs. Having established this pattern for about five years, he is invariably back to work by Monday handling his job responsibilities in a satisfactory way.

Leslie, a store manager, has an unusual agreement with his wife of 20 years. Providing he fulfills his financial obligations to the family, takes care of her sexual needs, and does not tell the neighbors about his way of having a *little after-hours fun,* he can wear her clothes as often as he likes. Leslie is a transvestite with no apparent qualms about his behavioral peculiarity. When he feels the urge to wear female attire outside his home, Leslie does so in a circumspect manner. He packs a suitcase with his change of clothing and travels to a section of town where he is unlikely to be seen by family, friends, or company employees.

Midge is a middle manager in a life insurance company. Skillful in financial matters, she has an investment that is currently yielding a 90 percent return on investment. Midge is a slumlord on a moderate scale. She owns two buildings more suitable for demolition than occupancy. Midge has been able to avoid reprisals by the city because her tenants are mostly foreign-speaking individuals who are unaware of their avenues of recourse. Of little concern to Midge is the inconsistency between her off-the-job occupation and the company objective of improving the quality of life in the United States.

Assuming their respective managements become aware of the off-hours activities of Mike, Leslie, and Midge, should they intervene? Would it be proper for management to attempt to bring all forms of deviancy under control, even if the particular form of deviancy had no bearing on on-the-job effectiveness? As stated earlier, my opinion is that deviant behavior patterns relating to personal and sexual life (providing they are unrelated to job effectiveness) remain the private concern of individuals. Management has no right, for example, to insist that all its employees maintain a heterosexual preference or abstain from smoking marijuana.

Cases of value deviance—such as that of Midge—where an individual's off-the-job activities are in diametrical conflict with organizational purposes and goals, might be considered from a different perspective. Hospitals have a right to insist that their employees do not deliberately spread disease during off hours; banks have a right to insist that their employees do not serve as loan sharks on the weekend, and colleges have a right to disallow their employees from staffing "diploma mills" at night. With these exceptions withstanding, management has the compelling problem remaining of identifying organizational members who practice deviancy during working hours.

11

Who Should Blow the Whistle?

Every person who feels that his or her job responsibility transcends the narrow confines of a job description or set of objectives shares the responsibility for combating managerial deviance. Nobody whose work directly or indirectly involves making an organization more productive, efficient, or humane should neglect the urgent task of exposing unethical, immoral, or even unsavory actions on the part of management. The people most directly influenced by managerial deviancy are precisely those who should bring such behavior to the attention of somebody with sufficent power to rectify the situation.

What are the unstated implications of having whistle-blowers implanted throughout the organization? Are we calling for a witch hunt, a gestapo-like investigation, to rid the organization of misfits, miscreants, and perhaps a few innocent managers in the process? Only by exposing deviant behavior from a number of vantage points can the spread of deviance be controlled. Exposing significant acts of deviancy is no more of a witch hunt than exposing fire hazards, leaking pipes, or open safes.

What about the good old-fashioned virtue of "loyalty to the boss and company?" Would it not be disloyal for a subordinate to report to the company president that his or her boss was asking people in the department for rebates on salary increases? Would it not be disloyal for a production worker in a toy factory to write a note to his or her congressman that the company continues to produce flammable toys despite protests from within? These are acts of *loyalty*, not disloyalty, if the long-term welfare of the organization is the paramount consideration.

Evaluation by Superiors

Managers have an ongoing responsibility as whistleblowers about deviance. Whenever a boss detects deviant behavior in a subordinate, he must take some constructive action. What kind of constructive action to take has been described in the chapters dealing with confronting deviant behavior, developing a strategic plan, rewarding nondeviant behavior, and discouraging deviant behavior.

Realistically, there will be instances in which a careful following of the plan elucidated will still not quell deviant behavior in a given subordinate. Many managers have asked me: "Okay, how long does an organization have to put up with an alcoholic (or any other form of maladaptive behavior)? We tried everything with this guy, but nothing seems to work. He seems to shape up for a few weeks, but then the least little thing goes wrong at home or on the job and he's back off the wagon again." Extenuating circumstances (such as a severe personal tragedy or physical illness) must be considered, but it would appear that most forms of managerial deviance should not be tolerated more than a few months after the initial confrontation. Some progress in overcoming deviant behavior should be made almost immediately, and substantial progress, within one or two months. Three to five months might be considered the outer limit to allow traces of deviant behavior to remain. Continued instances of managerial deviance beyond that time frame should be grounds for dismissal.

A superior is a whistle-blower about deviant subordinates because he or she alerts both the subordinate and *other members of the organization* about the observed deviance. Beyond an initial warning, managerial deviancy should not be kept a secret. A manager working with a subordinate to help him modify deviant behavior should inform his own boss and perhaps a representative of the personnel department about this activity. Deviant behavior and its remedial plans should be brought out into the open.

Evaluation by Peers

Assistant Vice-President. Elaine was promoted to assistant vice-president of student affairs, something that would never have happened if the vice-president knew how she really operates. I know the college was looking to promote a woman into that position, but they could have made a much better choice. Elaine is really an imposter, not a contributor.

I'll explain what I mean about being an imposter. First of all, Elaine has no professional skills. She doesn't belong in a job like that. Whenever she has to write a memo or a report she gets somebody else to do it for her. She's tricky enough to have somebody from outside her department write her reports. Elaine would be afraid of being exposed by secretaries in her own department. You should see Elaine in a meeting. The only contribution she makes is to flirt with the men. Other people are trying to get something serious accomplished and Elaine diverts attention away from the task with her flirting.

Her naive approaches to winning a battle for her department are nauseating even if they have worked a few times. She pulls the "helpless, innocent little girl" routine to get what she wants. Male chauvinists love her approach; it fits into their stereotype of how an attractive women conducts business.

Elaine's boss promoted her because he really didn't understand her lack of qualifications for the job. If he had only asked the people who work with Elaine, we would have saved him the embarrassment of putting a devious loser like her into an important position in the college.

Peer or buddy ratings have some merit in preventing managerial deviants like Elaine from receiving unwarranted promotions. Peers are usually more familiar with the day-to-day actions of a worker than is his or her boss. Coworkers are often acutely aware that deviant behavior is taking place long before the boss recognizes that a problem exists. Peers also have more exposure to the errant behavior of each other than does the boss. Before further extolling the virtues of peer ratings or evaluations in detecting deviance, two natural shortcomings of such a system are worth mentioning.[1]

For one thing, people at the same management level may be friends or rivals. If friends, there is a natural tendency not to report to management—even if requested—wrongdoings that could lead to reprisals for a friend. Friends tend to be protective of each other in a job environment. In the latter instance, reports of deviant behavior may be exaggerated in order for one rival to win out over another in the competition for promotion. Another inherent disadvantage to any system of peer evaluation is that some parties make an informal pact to describe each other to management only in a favorable light.

An effective system of peer review asks coworkers to both rate each other on standard rating scales and to write a few descriptive statements about each other. Questions of this nature might be: "Describe in a few sentences what you think are this person's strong points as they relate to the job." "Describe in a few sentences what you think this person's weak points might be as they relate to the job. Give a specific example if you can." Comments made in response to the latter question may provide a clue to possible deviant behaviors. A statement made by one individual about another should never be considered definitive evidence of managerial deviancy, but when the same deviant behavior has been mentioned several times, there is a legitimate problem. Often different statements may refer to the same behavior.

For instance, all the following peer comments may refer to a case of pathological lying:

"Not the most straightforward person I've worked with."

"I get the impression that he's hiding something."

"No real weakness, but we nickname him Janus."

"If he told me the time, I'd check it out with another person before I would set my watch by it."

"Has an unusual sense of humor. You never know if he is kidding or telling the truth."

The equivalent of peer review can be achieved by the existence of a leadership climate that welcomes criticism of people at all organizational levels. A boss that actually welcomes being made aware of problems by his or her actions gains the advantage of peer evaluation. Cliff, a partner in a certified public accounting firm, established such a climate. At the end of a performance evaluation, he asked Al if there were any problems that management could help him with. Al replied:

> I'm glad you asked. I feel uneasy telling you about what's wrong with somebody else at my level, but we have one hornet's nest of a problem on our hands. Jeff, one of the auditors on my team, is putting himself and our firm in a very bad light. Two different people in client firms have asked me if my friend is feeling all right. Just yesterday I was asked if Jeff has a drinking problem. But it's not only the drinking. He appears so distracted when we're at a client's that people tend to ignore his requests. I've asked Jeff if he has a drinking problem. He has told me twice that he sometimes appears drowsy because of some allergy shots that he has been taking. I dislike being an informant but something has to be done.

Evaluation by Subordinates

Subordinates are another logical source of evaluation comments in assessing the capabilities and growth potential

of a manager. For several reasons, infrequent use has been
made of this promising source of information about managerial competence. For one, a widely accepted principle in
most organizations is that those with higher rank evaluate
the competence of those with lower rank. The more formal
power a person has (the higher rank) the more weight is giv-
en to his or her evaluation of another organization member.
John B. Miner notes other limitations to subordinate evaluation of superiors:

> Where subordinates are asked to evaluate their superi-
> ors, other problems arise. The anticipation of reprisal,
> whether justified or not, means that only the reckless or
> those who are on the verge of quitting may be willing to
> express a negative opinion. Furthermore, subordinates
> are likely to have personal objectives that differ from
> corporate objectives and that may exert an undue influ-
> ence on the ratings.[2]

Robert Hershey has developed an approach to subordinate evaluation that is well suited for detecting managerial
deviancy. Observations about deviant behavior are made in
the process of collecting information for other appraisal purposes. Hershey notes that whenever subordinate ratings are
turned in to company personnel, the confidentiality of any
comments are suspected and therefore inhibited. "The subordinate who might give his boss an unflattering rating—or
point to deviant behavior—would hesitate, if he or she knew
that these ratings might leak back to the manager
evaluated."[3]

According to Hersey, the most effective approach lies in
contracting for the services of an outside professional—a
consulting psychologist, attorney, or management consultant. The outsider must be above reproach and have no links
to either the corporate personnel department or line management. The outside evaluator is interested in characteristics
that could be crucial for management performance including instances of emotional disorder or deviancy.

Actually, evaluator is the wrong word; the consultant is
a collector. He asks subordinates (not peers) such questions as, "What are his strong and weak points?",
"Where can he improve himself?", "What kind of boss
is he?", etc. The point is to provide the ratee's boss with
additional inputs. This "over and under" approach (one
level over the ratee, one under) would provide the primary rater—the manager's boss—with a subordinate's
eye view of the man being rated.[4]

Which technique to use to contact subordinates in the interest of confidentiality must be worked out by each organization. Sometimes the consultant is provided with the
names and home telephone or office extensions of the subordinates. He would then randomly pick three names (or use
all the names) and ask each person to call him back at a number that had been previously announced as an "appraisal"
number. An overall appraisal report could then be fed back
to both the person being rated and his or her boss. People resist evaluation less when they have an opportunity to see the
evaluation results. Such an approach also rests on firmer ethical (and recently, legal) footing than showing a person's
appraisal only to the superior.

Another approach would be for the consultant to administer a rating form with both attitudes scale items and open-
ended questions to all of the executive's subordinates. Two
useful open-ended questions here are: "In what way is this
manager particularly effective?" and "In what way is this
manager unusually poor or ineffective?" People sometimes
provide rich information to open-ended questions while answering rating scale items in a haphazard, unconcerned
manner. Many colleges and universities use this technique
for student evaluation of faculty, leading Hershey to conclude: "there are no reasons why it cannot be employed in
an industrial setting."

Managers who resist being evaluated by their own subordinates in general are precisely those people with the most
to hide from their superiors. A claim of "invasion of priva-

cy" is difficult to justify because a manager is not asked to provide any information about himself or herself. He or she stands on the behavior previously exhibited to subordinates! As one self-confident, almost brash, R&D manager commented about subordinate evaluation: "Ask any of my people anything you want about me. If a manager can't take evaluation by his people, a chef shouldn't be able to stand evaluation by his customers."

Impromptu Exposure

Frank Serpico, the incorruptable policeman hero in the Peter Maas novel, is an idealized version of a deviance worker. Serpico was willing to accept physical and psychological abuse, including thinly veiled threats of death, in order to expose deviance in his organization—the New York City Police Department. This case of "the honest cop who blew the whistle" dramatically describes how a worker at any level in an organization can try to expose deviance through informal channels. Serpico singlehandedly brought a scandal to public attention that led to the formation of the Knapp Commission, a task force charged with investigating corruption in the NYPD.

For several years policeman Serpico had been unable to find an honest, responsible official who would listen to his tale of pervasive corruption among his fellow policemen. Frustrated and running out of alternatives, Serpico told his story to the *New York Times.* When word was picked up that the *Times* was about to print Serpico's story, Mayor John Lindsay appointed the Knapp Commission. Although all managerial deviance in the New York City Police Department may not now be eradicated, Frank Serpico has illustrated that a person at any organizational level can expose ethical deviance.

A growing number of workers in corporate life have followed Serpico's lead of exposing misdeeds by management.[5] Perhaps the most dramatic example was the unidentified ITT employee who presented columnist Jack Anderson with the Dita Beard and Chile memos. Another example of whistle-blowing, and a vehicle for further whistle-blowing, are described by *Time*:

> . . . Recently Robert Rowen, a former nuclear control technician at Pacific Gas & Electric Co., filed 49 charges against the utility with the Atomic Energy Commission: he alleged that P.G.& E. deliberately violated Government safety regulations in handling radioactive waste. The AEC later sustained two of the charges and rebuked the company on several more.
>
> Consumer Advocate Ralph Nader has formed an organization for corporate tattletales called the Clearing House for Professional Responsibility. . . . It is hiring a full-time employment counselor to help them find new jobs if they are fired, and even has a special mail drop to receive anonymous tips: P.O. Box 486, Benjamin Franklin Station, Washington, D.C. 20044. . . .

An individual who is not able to bring about the reversal of an unethical practice by speaking to officials within his or her corporation now has a sympathetic ear outside the organization. Before using the power of an outside consumer group to overcome deviance, several preliminary steps should be exhausted. As the process is described by *Time*:

> *Going Public.* Once a worker decides to speak up, how should he go about it? Ralph Nader advises him first to "appeal internally" to his superiors, moving up the chain of command until he produces results. If he runs into a dead end, and if the consequences of continued wrong practice "will result in further injury, fraud or other corporate or governmental crime against consumers," a worker should go public—by contacting the press, his Congressman or his Senator. Nader cautions dissident employees to resist resigning from the company if at all possible. "If you go," he asks, "who remains to fight the good fight?"
>
> Mortimer Feinberg, professor of industrial psycholo-

gy at the City University of New York, recommends five steps for conscience-stricken workers:

Report the problem to an immediate supervisor.

If the supervisor does not act, ask his permission to make a statement to the company president.

If the statement produces no results, write a letter to the firm's vice president for public relations, who often is the voice of the public within the company and may be able to move the president.

If there is still no reaction to the complaint, and the matter is too serious to forget, submit a written resignation specifying the reasons.

At this point it is perfectly ethical to take the case to the public. But make certain that the case is strong and well documented.[6]

A less formal and much tamer procedure for blowing the whistle on managerial deviance is to write an anonymous letter of complaint to the deviant manager involved. If that letter does not result in a change in behavior (elimination of the deviant practice), send a letter to the deviant's boss. Sue, a computer programmer, provides a simple example of how this process works:

> The problem we were having in our department was that Jack, our manager, was rarely around when we needed him. When he was around, his advice on technical or administrative problems was pretty good. Nobody in the department knew for sure where Jack went on his long lunches or mysterious absences, but we suspected he was tending to another business on the side. The anonymous letter routine worked very well.
>
> I wrote Jack a letter for the group stating something like: "You're a competent boss when we can find you. If you would drop by the office a little bit more, it would make it much easier for us to do our job." Jack began almost immediately to spend most of his time in the department. In a staff meeting two weeks later, he announced: "My special task force assignment is now

winding down. I know that some of you have been concerned that I haven't devoted enough time to this department's responsibilities. The confidential problems that kept me away are now resolved." Whether or not Jack was telling the truth is incidental. What is important is that he is now doing his fair share of work as a manager.

What About Reprisals?

Whistle-blowers are not well received by all members of top management, nor is anybody who turns in an unfavorable report on the competence of a peer or subordinate. James M. Roche, former chairman of General Motors, said in a speech:

> Some of the enemies of business now encourage an employee to be disloyal to the enterprise. They want to create suspicion and disharmony. However this is labeled—industrial espionage, whistle blowing, or professional responsibility—it is another tactic for spreading disunity and creating conflict.[7]

Many employees have been fired, demoted, or forced to resign because they have actively opposed corporate policy they felt was unethical or deviant in some other way. A United States Steel Company sales executive in Texas went over his superiors' head to object to company officers about defective pipe tubing ready to be marketed by the giant steel manufacturer. Company officials investigated the situation, withdrew the piping, and fired the sales executive.

Despite the risks involved in reporting deviant behavior to top management or an agency outside the organization, there are instances in which blowing the whistle on deviance is rewarded. As more organizations learn that reporting on instances of management neglect (when the consequences are serious) can have long-range benefits, whistle-blowers are less likely to be punished by their own organization. Edward A. Gregory, a body shop inspector employed by General Motors, filed a complaint with Ralph Nader after his management refused to acknowledge his admonitions about a carbon monoxide leak in some Chevrolet bodies.[8] In addition, Gregory was transferred to another assignment. Nader and Gregory then publicized the defect and G.M. was forced to recall 3,000,000 Chevrolet cars that year. G.M. lavished rewards on Gregory in the form of (a) a $10,000 United States savings bond for the suggestion that helped repair the defect, (b) a reinstatement to his old job, (c) paying closer attention to his technical observations. He has since pointed out other defects that led to the recall of 4,000,000 additional cars.

Project Engineer. A less dramatic and sizeable, but still meaningful, reward forthcoming to a whistle-blower is that associated with the feeling of accomplishing something important for the organization. Any person with a commitment to organizational efficiency (or justice) can get a psychic kick out of exposing managerial deviance. Tony, a project engineer, reports a straightforward case example of how this principle operates:

> Barney, our boss, had gradually retreated into his own little dream world. He was so intent on becoming a company president that he neglected the very task that might allow him to become a president. He was so busy dreaming up grand schemes and playing politics that he neglected to function as a chief engineer. Delegation became an obsession for Barney. When you finally got an appointment with him, he would assign you more of his work rather than trying to help you with your problem or give you a needed decision.
>
> It was bad enough that Barney was pulling down a high salary for doing very little. Even worse was that he was preventing the project engineer from getting their projects completed. He served as a block to progress since things like budgets and hiring authorizations still had to be cleared through him. Finally I went to the company president with the whole story. Our president

listened for 30 minutes, then said: "I'm glad you brought this problem to our attention. We were beginning to think that something was wrong in your department." Barney has since departed to run his own little job shop. His quest for power is now satisfied, but more important to me is that our department now runs like a first-class outfit.

12

Counterstatements

Any systematic approach to changing human behavior or attitudes including psychoanalysis, transcendental meditation, or even management simulation games will encounter both skepticism and criticism. Similarly, the basic ideas presented in this book are unlikely to meet with universal approval. An unknown number of managers, management scientists, behavioral scientists, religious workers, and a few managerial deviants themselves will probably take exception to the basic thrust of these ideas. Next, we will examine some of these anticipated counterstatements. By doing so, it is hoped to both answer some probable criticism and clarify further the key ideas underlying my prescription for the control of managerial deviance.

The Great Jackass Fallacy

Harry Levinson has scored management for its widespread belief in "the great jackass fallacy." Any organization, according to Levinson, that attempts to motivate people by the manipulation of rewards and punishments (as suggested here) entertains this "jackass fallacy." Reports Levinson:

Frequently, I have asked executives this question: What is the dominant philosophy of motivation in American management? Almost invariably, they quickly agree that it is the carrot-and-stick philosophy, reward and punishment. Then I ask them to close their eyes for a moment, and form a picture in their mind's eye with a carrot at one end and a stick at the other. When they have done so, I then ask them to describe the central image in that picture. Most frequently they respond that the central figure is a jackass.

If the first image that comes to mind when one thinks "carrot-and-stick" is a jackass, then obviously the unconscious assumption behind the reward-punishment model is the one dealing with jackasses who must be manipulated and controlled. Thus, unconsciously, the boss is the manipulator and controller, and the subordinate is the jackass.[1]

As an alternative to the reward-and-punishment model, Levinson urges management to use a *psychological* conception of people. Each person has a unique set of motives, needs, and ideals. He sees most of people's wrongdoing in organizations (for example, sloppy work, absenteeism, undermotivation) stemming from anger and a need to protect themselves. To protect their self-esteem against a carrot-and-stick philosophy and the hierarchical organization, many people fight back by producing shoddy work and leaving jobs.

Although my plan for combatting aberrant behavior emphasizes the systematic dispensing of rewards (and some mild punishments if this doesn't work), it does not exclude the premise that people have complicated motivational makeups. Assume that an organization learns that the manufacturing head continues to use aerosol products emitting the toxic substance, vinyl chloride (despite his knowledge of their harmful effects on people). His management can probably induce him to stop using these aerosols by confronting him with the problem and rewarding him for making the change. This procedure will work (induce the manager to be less deviant) for a variety of motives that could explain why the manufacturing head uses dangerous chemicals. The same technique will work for changing his actions, whether the manager is using hazardous aerosols because (a) he is more concerned about organizational efficiency than human suffering, (b) he has a deep-rooted need to strike back at management for having imposed a multilayerd hierarchy over his head, or (c) he is craving attention.

The same principle applies in psychotherapy. Psychotherapists, particularly those with a psychoanalytic bent, are the professional mental health workers most likely to examine complicated motivational patterns in their patients. In trying to help their patients change behavior, however, very few therapists match different techniques to different motives. For instance, almost every patient might be confronted with the illogic of some of his or her actions and then receive reassurance (positive motivator) when he or she does something logical.

Despite the complexity of human motivation, it is a universal principle that people do things (including changing their behavior in a nondeviant direction) in response to appropriate rewards. One compulsive gambler may stop spending working hours at the track (or on the phone with his stockbroker) if he has the chance to earn more money through his work. Another compulsive gambler might curtail his gambling if only management would *stroke* him (give him more attention). A third compulsive gambler might attend more to his job if transferred to a more exciting (challenging) form of work. Each compulsive gambler had a different reason for gambling on company time—one out of financial need, one out of desire for attention, the third out of boredom. Nevertheless, they all modify their behavior in response to an appropriate (one that fits) reward.

Management Is Not the Practice of Psychotherapy

A manager should not attempt to function as a psychiatrist, psychologist, or psychotherapist on the job. Neither should a personnel specialist or trainer. My system does not require a manager to administer psychological treatment to deviant people. An important premise of the plan is that managers who require (or who might require) professional mental health assistance should be strongly encouraged to seek such help. The manager-as-behavior-modifier fits in a dispenser of rewards for significant instances of nondeviant behavior. He or she is not competing with the outside interventionist who is working professionally with the managerial deviant.

In this scheme, the manager is not even asked to become a specially trained *behavior modification technologist* or *contingency manager.* He or she may require some training about systematically coaching subordinates—something that any effective manager should know. However, following my plan, the manager is not required to make detailed recordings of behavioral events or to dispense M&M candy, or half-dollars, on an hourly basis. Anyone who has worked himself into a responsible managerial position can recognize a change from deviant to nondeviant behavior without keeping detailed logs.

Managers Are Not Retards, Psychotics, Delinquents, Schoolchildren, Rats, or Pigeons

Applications of behavior modification have been generally accomplished so far in isolated organizational settings and with limited groups. Many of the experiments and field applications of applied behavioral analysis (yet another synonym for behavior modification) have even been accomplished with infrahuman organisms. The basic principles underlying behaviorism (the science on which behavior modification is based) come from experimentation with rats and pigeons.

With these observations in mind, it would not be surprising that many people think behavior modification has limited applicability to managerial life. This argument is specious for two major reasons. For one, approaches to modifying behavior in settings such as hospitals, schoolrooms, and animal laboratories can only make use of a limited range of rewards. In my plan, managerial deviants will not be dispensed rewards such as food pellets, "points" that enable them to leave the company premises, or gold stars for good performance. All of these rewards may be appropriate in some settings, but they would not be appropriate for managers and staff people. As described above, my approach uses a wide range of meaningful rewards. Correspondingly, punishments—when used—involve factors such as demotion, criticism, and the withholding of managerial privileges, not the use of mild electric shocks or withholding of pudding for dessert.

Of greater significance, the application of behavior modification in business and industry has already produced some dramatic results, both in training supervisors and in raising the productivity of a variety of people.[2] Industrial applications such as these would strongly suggest that applied behavioral analysis has relevance for groups other than patients, prisoners, schoolchildren, and infrahumans. Edward J. Feeney, a vice-president at Emery Air Freight Corporation, has pioneered in the application of contingency management to improving organizational efficiency. A sampling of the results his company has achieved are quoted from *Business Week:*

. . . Feeney devised a simple checklist to let each employee determine for himself how well the goals were being met. At the same time, supervisors and regional sales managers applied positive reinforcement in the form of praise and recognition for performance improvement. The results: Container use throughout the country jumped from 45 percent to 95 percent. And in more than 70 percent of the offices, the increase came in a single day.

More important, performance has remained at this high level for nearly two years. In the few cases in which feedback was temporarily interrupted because of, for example, managerial changes, performance slumped more than 50 percent, only to rise rapidly when feedback was resumed. Cost reduction from the program was initially pegged at $650,000 a year, but in October alone, record savings of $125,000 were chalked up.[3]

Manipulation Is a Deviant Act Itself

Contingency management—the least emotional of all terms referring to behavior modification—involves the manipulation of factors in the environment (rewards and punishment) to induce an individual to behave in a particular way. Even if that "particular way" happens to be something that helps the organization and society, such as nondeviant behavior, many people strenuously object to the very concept of *manipulation*. In the perception of many people, manipulation is a deviant act. My system thus uses one form of deviant behavior (contingency management) to combat managerial deviance. Similarly, policemen often resort to violence in order to quell violence; parents often yell at children in order to quiet them. People themselves sometimes object to receiving rewards contingent upon their behavior. Brian, an organization development specialist in a large business, commented:

> I wish the hell Paul would cut out that behavior-mod-type stuff. It seems that whenever I say something or do something Paul thinks is good, he smiles and nods his head. When I make a statement that he feels is wrong or reflects a wrong attitude on my part, he reacts to me with a blank stare or a grimace of disapproval. I know what Paul is doing and why he's doing it. Despite my knowledge of what's going on, I think he does influence my actions.

Brian, similar to many people, objects to a technology of human behavior that actually works. People running for political office, for instance, often get upset about scientifically conducted opinion polls because polls so conducted have an enviable track record. Politicians get much less upset about predictions by their opponents because such public predictions are usually an admixture of subjective judgment and wishful thinking. What most people fail to acknowledge is that contingency management merely substitutes a systematic approach of modifying behavior with an unsystematic, random approach. It appears that the majority of people feel the morally correct method of changing behavior is through exhortation and appeal to values or through the universal application of financial incentives. Despite this belief, appeals to decency or citizenship or the vague promise of earning more money, often fail to motivate people. These approaches fail because the person soon learns that the effort they expend is not closely related to any particular reward.

A letter written to the editor of the *American Psychological Association Monitor* cogently expresses the position that the alternative to behavior modification (in a variety of settings) is not the absence of people trying to manipulate the behavior of each other. John M. Throne of the University of Kansas writes:

> The latest series of flaps over behavior modification highlights the unavoidability of certain fundamental socio-political, as well as scientific facts. Behavior is always being modified. Like it or not, the evidence is that each society's members have no choice but to modify one another's behavior. The means employed need not (though, of course, they may) include authoritarian steps taken without regard to the deserving interests of all who are participants in the society. Democratic steps can be weaved into a society's fabric as well as authoritarian, though perhaps less easily; at least this is what the U.S. experiment has been all about for 200 years, is it not? . . .[4]

Nondeviant Behavior Might be Modified Next

At this writing, the year 1984 is less than a decade away. Many people feel that a widespread use of behavior control will move society rapidly toward the authoritarian conditions described in *1984*. What might happen if those attempting to control managerial deviance become really effective in accomplishing their mission? Might they not then try out these newly developed behavior modification skills on people who are not deviant? Wouldn't a lot of people whose behavior did not require control be manipulated into behaving in ways deemed appropriate by management?

On the surface, this concern seems quite reasonable. It would appear that a small group of people might control the behavior of many others to serve their own ends. Contingency management, however, does not operate like flouridation of water or mass vaccination.

Correctly modifying the behavior of another individual (motivating him or her) requires a delicate one-to-one relationship.[5] One person has to observe desirable and undesirable behavior in another individual and then administer an appropriate reward or punishment. The general scheme advanced here of systematically encouraging productive (nondeviant) behavior would indeed be worthwhile if applied to a wider range of people than managerial deviants. Astute managers, coaches, teachers, psychotherapists, ministers, lawyers, and salespeople are already doing this intuitively. Effective leaders owe much of their effectiveness to their ability to encourage good performance.

Another way of expressing this same concern about one subgroup in the population modifying the behavior of many others is to ask "Who will control the controllers?" What assurances do we have that the allegedly nondeviant managers will not manipulate other people into doing rather devious things? Could it not be, for instance, that a company president might manipulate his vice-president of research and development into conducting corporate espionage in the service of the president's company?

One important flaw in the logic of those concerned about the wrong people obtaining control is the neglect of an important principle: people will only *continue to behave in ways that are reinforcing*. Only helpless individuals will stick around to endure punishment for long. Assume you and your boss are traveling together on a business trip. He praises you every time the speedometer on the car you are driving exceeds 55 miles per hour. Gradually, without realizing what is happening, you may accelerate past 55 miles per hour at every feasible opportunity. After a couple of hours of behaving in this modified way (assume that you were a conservative driver in the past), a state trooper flags you down and gives you a summons for speeding. Your modified behavior will quickly revert to a safer (more rewarding) pattern. Living organisms rarely continue to behave in ways that are punishing (unless by severe force). People will not continue to follow a leader who imposes a steady diet of aversive conditions on them—particularly in a job environment.

An unfortunate incident in an industrial parts factory illustrates how people quickly discard new behavior patterns that lead to aversive consequences. A woman production operator working on a piece rate incentive system was subject to machine-mediated behavior modification (which, of course, was originally programmed by a person). The more parts this woman punched per hour, the more pay she received. Situations like this tend to be addictive. Endowed with rapid reflexes, this woman was soon producing punched parts at a rate surpassing factory records for the job. Finally her rapid speed exceeded the delay interval required for safe operation. She lost the tips of two fingers at the moment of her peak performance. At her own request, after recuperation, this woman was transferred to a job with less emphasis on tying financial reward to performance.

Stockholders (or Taxpayers) Will Object

Public reaction to large-scale attempts at behavior modification in institutional settings have been met with disfavor by a variety of groups including the American Civil Liberties Union. People feel in general that deviant behavior should be dealt with only in conventional ways. Long-term incarceration, physical punishments or heavy fines are favored approaches to dealing with deviance. Civil libertari-

ans have been instrumental in getting the federal
government to back off from funding programs of behavior
modification in certain prisons. The ACLU has been particularly persistent in attacking a project of behavior control
funded by the Law Enforcement Assistance Administration.
Noteworthy is that the program of behavior modification under attack is based exclusively on positive motivators:

> The one-year-old project, described as a "contingency
> management program," is based on the token economy
> concept. It was designed by E. Scott Geller and Daniel
> F. Johnson, psychology professors at Virginia Poly-
> technic Institute and State University. The project was
> intended as a pilot program for Virginia's proposed
> maximum security facility. Its objectives, according to
> the operations manual are (1) "to receive inmates who
> are particularly troublesome to themselves, to other in-
> mates, and, thus, to the smooth administration of cor-
> rectional programs within the state system and (2) to
> modify the actions of such inmates so that they may be
> returned to the beneficial influence of correctional pro-
> grams in the general population of another institution
> until their sentences are fulfilled."
> Designed to operate in four graduated stages, the pro-
> gram is now being conducted in the maximum security
> padlock cells at the state penitentiary in Richmond and
> the state farm in Goochland County. The only inmates
> eligible for the program are those who "represent the
> greatest security risk and the greatest potential for dis-
> rupting traditional treatment programs." The psycholo-
> gists who administer the program emphasize that it is
> completely voluntary and that it aims to reach its objec-
> tives through the use of "positive reinforcers" only.
> An inmate who volunteers to participate in the con-
> tingency management program may enter State I by
> CMP credit card. He may then "earn" credits by keep-
> ing his cell neat, his face clean, his hair combed and his
> shirt buttoned. He must also follow uncomplainingly
> such administrative procedures as daily counts and

shakedowns, and "engage in civil interactions" with the guards and CMP counselors. The counselors, most of whom have BA's in psychology, enter the credits on plastic punch cards that can later be used to purchase commissary items or to rent recreational materials.

If counselors and prison administrators agree that an inmate's behavior has improved sufficiently, he moves into Stage II at the state farm, where he has a little more freedom of movement and more behavioral requirements. Stages III and IV are located at a correctional unit where inmates can get typing and keypunch training. By Stage IV, an inmate is to receive actual money (rather than plastic credits) for work in data processing.

After Stage IV—the inmate is presumably "rehabilitated" enough to return to the general population at the state penitentiary—where, however, the behavioral skills he learned in the CMP may or may not be reinforced.

Despite the constructive sound of the plan, the Virginia program has been sharply criticized by the ACLU's National Prison Project for its emphasis on "institutionalization." "The object of this program," says National Prison Project attorney Arpiar Saunders, "is to make the prisoners obedient and passive. It was designed for purposes of management and control."[6]

A systematic plan for combatting deviant behavior in management might similarly be accused of aiming at management and control. Management and control directed toward constructive (and away from destructive) ends, however, is useful to society. My prescription for dealing with managerial deviance would be less subject to attack by the ACLU (or lawyers in general) because it is less contrived and mechanical. Also it is not imposed on a group of people involuntarily belonging to an institution (such as a prison or elementary school setting). Under the plan, the alcoholic vice-president of marketing is not asked to flash his "contingency management card" and receive a credit whenever he comes back sober from lunch. Instead, his boss might make verbal mention of a good idea the vice-president contributes to a staff meeting conducted immediately after lunch. If drunk, as in the past, this contribution might not have been made.

Managers Shouldn't Require Positive Reinforcement to Behave in Nondeviant Ways

Understandably, many people would object to the concept of rewarding nondeviant behavior exhibited by formerly deviant managers while the majority of managers go about behaving normally without any particular reward. Critics of my plan might comment: "Should a member of Congress who does not lie, a businessman who does not produce unsafe products, or a physician who avoids malpractice be singled out for reward?" My answer is that most people find sufficient reward in behaving in nondeviant ways. The member of Congress might get a bang out of passing useful legislation; the ethical businessman might find the accumulation of goodwill appealing; and the physician might find ample reward in helping people. Laying on verbal praise (or other forms of additional reward) is superfluous.

B. F. Skinner, perhaps the most influential figure in the behavior modification movement, attributes much of the criticism of his work (and the ineffectiveness of many of our social programs) to the nonscientific concept, *should.* Similarly, John Cline, the project director for a performance contract in public education, has expressed exasperation with criticism of the use of rewards to reinforce classroom learning: "We hear from people that the kid should *want* to succeed. Well, goddamn yeah, he *should.* But he doesn't."[7]

Similarly, managers and professional people should not behave in deviant ways, but occasionally they do. Lectures about the importance of not being deviant meet with limited success in bringing about changes in behavior. A moral deviant who uses electronic bugging devices to obtain trade secrets already knows that such an approach to gathering information about competitive products is immoral (if not illegal). A psychopathic liar who tells his subordinates anything to placate them also recognizes that such actions fall outside the limits of ethical behavior. Managerial deviants *should* not behave in nefarious ways, but they do. Thus the need for a program of contingency management.

Nothing This Naive and Simplistic Will Work

The most vitriolic criticism of my prescription for deviance will probably be that it is inelegant, simplistic, and naive; because of these factors it will not work. In overview, the plan for combatting managerial deviance involves confronting deviant people about their behavior and holding them accountable for the consequences of their subsequent actions. Progress toward constructive, functional behavior is given positive reinforcement. If deviant behavior persists, negative reinforcement and punishment are administered. Among the complexities of the plan are: (a) choosing a realistic incentive that turns that person on, and (b) if necessary, finding a punishment that does not humiliate the individual or turn him away from the organization.

Evidence that such a prescription will help alleviate the contemporary problem of managerial deviance comes from several unrelated sets of human interaction. Psychotherapy that results in actual changes in behavior characteristically includes the therapist confronting the patient or client with the self-defeating aspects of his or her behavior. When the person so confronted attempts a new form of behavior in the world outside the therapist's office and it *works*, he or she will probably repeat that newly learned behavior. Effective athletic coaches have practiced contingency management long before behavioral scientists provided a label and a package for this phenomenon. A place kicker approaching the ball at the wrong angle is quickly confronted with his mistake. He receives immediate praise in practice for straightening out the kick. During the game, his reward is clear-cut: points scored or yards not surrendered to the opposition. If verbal encouragement does not work, negative reinforcement is administered; the player will be removed from the game until he improves his place kicking skill.

Effective managers have inadvertently functioned as applied behavioral analysts, or contingency managers, as long as the art of management has been practiced. Implementing the coaching skills drummed into them by the rigors of trial and error, they have systematically confronted subordinates with their deviant ways and encouraged them toward more constructive modes of behavior. Capitalizing on successful strategies of this nature and refinements offered by behavioral science, today's manager can make a vital inroad toward diminishing the pernicious impact of deviant behavior in work organizations.

13

Sources of Help

A person attempting to overcome deviant behavior in management can find some assistance from professional helpers, organizations designed to combat specific forms of deviance, and training seminars. In addition, a body of written information has accumulated that can provide insight, understanding, and suggest necessary skills for waging the battle against deviant behavior in management. No manager can rightfully claim today that "nothing can be done about the problem of managerial deviance." Help is available.

Professional Help

Many forms of managerial deviance are essentially personality disorders. Managerial deviants should thus be encouraged to participate in individual or group psychotherapy. Standard sources of information such as telephone directories provide the names of certified psychologists and psychiatrists. Company physicians, county medical societies, or state psychological associations also maintain a listing of local mental health practitioners. A good starting point for the rehabilitation of a deviant whose problems involve medical complications (for example, alcoholism and other addictions) is referral to a physician. A company doctor is much more likely to provide feedback to management than is a private physician hired by the managerial deviant.

Organizations Designed to Provide Assistance

A number of organizations have been founded to help people cope with specific forms of deviant behavior. Frequently they provide the deviant individual an experience that leads eventually to recovery. Organizations of this nature cannot help every deviant conquer his or her form of maladaptive behavior. Many deviants do not want to be helped (in behavioristic terms, substitute "do not find nondeviant behavior rewarding" for "do not want to be helped").

Alcoholics Anonymous is widely recognized as the single most effective aid in the recovery of an alcoholic. Virtually every community in the country has a chapter. "AA is a fellowship of men and women which works directly with the individual, and the only requirement for membership is a desire by the individual to stop drinking. Its assistance is given promptly and willingly to anyone who asks for help. There are no dues or fees."

Among the members of AA are many managerial and professional people. For further information consult your local telephone directory or write, Alcoholics Anonymous, Post Office Box 459, Grand Central Station, New York, N.Y. 10017.

Al-Anon Family Groups are closely aligned to the mission of AA, although not directly connected with AA. Al-Anon is a resource for the nonalcoholic family member, thus indirectly benefiting the alcoholic person. Wives or husbands of alcoholic managerial deviants might be interested in joining Al-Anon. Local chapters can be located through AA or the telephone directory, or write, The Al-Anon Family Group Headquarters, P.O. Box 182, Madison Square Station, New York, N.Y. 10010.

Gamblers Anonymous provides help to the compulsive gamblers in ways similar to those of Alcoholics Anonymous.

Founded in 1957, and now with chapters throughout the United States, GA is a "Fellowship of men and women who have joined together in order that they may stop gambling and to help other compulsive gamblers to do the same." Consult local listings or write P.O. Box 17173, Los Angeles, California 90017.

Gam-Anon, similar in philosophy to Al-Anon, is designed to help husbands, wives, relatives, and close friends of compulsive gamblers. An important objective of this organization is to help members better understand the compulsive gambler and to learn to cope with problems involved. Gam-Anon also provides ways to encourage the gambler to join Gamblers Anonymous and to help him or her achieve eventual recovery. Local chapters can be reached through their affiliation with Gamblers Anonymous or write, Gam-Anon, P.O. Box 4549, Downey, California 90241.

The National Council on Alcoholism, Inc. is the national voluntary health and information agency in the field of alcoholism. NCA provides information through a Labor-Management Service Department. Affiliated councils of this organization are located in over 80 communities. Several of the larger councils have special committees which work with business and industrial firms. Alcoholism Information Centers, operated by the councils provide a variety of functions including (a) liaison with Alcoholics Anonymous, (b) information and counseling to individuals, families and employers, (c) conducting public education programs about alcoholism. For further information write The National Council On Alcoholism, Inc., 2 Park Avenue, New York, N.Y. 10016.

The National Loss Control Service Corporation is a private management consulting firm located in physical proximity to the home office of the Kemper Insurance Companies. "Among its services for corporate and governmental organizations, it provides surveys on alcoholism and other behavioral problems, consultation on control program development, and evaluations of existing behavioral loss reduction procedures." The address of NATLSCO is Long Grove, Illinois 60049.

Odyssey House is an agency operating a group of private

treatment centers for narcotics addicts. Services of this agency include (a) nine residential therapeutic communities in four states concerned with attitudinal and behavioral rehabilitation, (b) a drug information and education division, (c) a training program for professionals working in the area of addiction, (d) community and ghetto medical programs. For information about their services of relevance to the drug addicted managerial deviant write, Odyssey House, 309–311 Sixth Street, New York, N.Y. 10003.

Synanon Foundation, originally an organization to help narcotic addicts overcome their addiction, has expanded to include alcoholics, other troubled persons, "and those who simply seek a drug-free, integrated and nonviolent community." The Synanon method of rehabilitation is based on the "straight talk" game and "a spirited verbal interaction." Run without a hired professional staff, Synanon aims at "turning out individuals who relate to each other as human beings, irrespective of poverty or wealth, skin-color, nationality, criminal or noncriminal background or any of the other partitions that tend to separate people." Its national headquarters is located at 1910 Ocean Front, Santa Monica, California 90406.

Workshops and Seminars

Systematically taking constructive action against managerial deviancy is an emerging phenomenon in organizational life. The American Management Association periodically runs seminars on topics such as "Alcoholism as a Management Problem," "Drugs as a Management Problem," or workshops on behavior modification. The AMA characteristically provides new seminars to match new concerns in management, increasing the chances that sessions will be run in the future about deviance control. For information write American Management Association, Inc., The American Management Association Building, 135 West 50th Street, New York, N.Y. 10020.

Development Dimensions, Inc., a private group of industrial psychologists and trainers, is now offering seminars designed to provide skill in behavior modification. Although not aimed directly at modifying deviant behavior, this seminar in "interaction modeling" (also known as "behavior modeling") could prove helpful in developing systematic coaching skills. For information about future seminars write Development Dimensions Inc., Suite 419, 250 Mt. Lebanon Boulevard, Pittsburgh, Pennsylvania 15234.

Pertinent Reading About Managerial Deviance

Notes to the chapters presented later suggest sources of additional information about the general problem of managerial deviance. The following list of books, articles, and pamphlets includes references already cited in this book plus additional information of benefit to people concerned about deviance detection and control.

American Psychiatric Association, *Behavior Therapy in Psychiatry,* explains in semitechnical detail the widespread application of behavior modification. Any manager with at least one course in abnormal psychology or its equivalent (who wants to learn about modifying behavior) will find this book helpful.

Paul Brodeur, *Expendable Americans,* Viking, 1974. An inside glimpse into an old form of managerial deviancy—allowing employees to work under physically hazardous conditions despite scientific evidence about the adverse consequences. Executives who recognize the problems created by substances such as asbestos but choose to ignore them, can be accused of this form of managerial deviancy.

Carl D. Chambers and Richard Heckman, *Employee Drug Abuse,* Cahners Books, 1974. A helpful examination of current information available about the drug problem in industry, plus some guidelines for the treatment and rehabilitation of drug abusers. Highly recommended for personnel directors and company physicians.

James C. Coleman, *Abnormal Psychology and Modern Life,* 4th edition, Scott, Foresman, 1972. Any manager or staff person attempting to deal with maladaptive behavior might profit from a review of basics. Aside from being relevant, this college text is well written and interesting. The chapters dealing with personality disorders and behavior therapy are particularly recommended to those concerned about managerial deviancy.

"Detour Alcoholism Ahead," Public Relations, Kemper Insurance Companies, Long Grove, Illinois 60049. A practical, straightforward pamphlet dealing with this form of deviant behavior.

Andrew J. DuBrin, *The Practice of Managerial Psychology*, Pergamon Press, 1972. The chapter on managerial obsolescence is particularly relevant to the problem of managerial deviance.

Andrew J. DuBrin, *Fundamentals of Organizational Behavior*, Pergamon Press, 1974. The chapters on improving employee performance, work motivation, and the future contain information geared toward understanding and controlling deviant behavior in organizations.

Arnold P. Goldstein and Melvin Sorcher, *Changing Supervisor Behavior*, Pergamon Press, 1974. Although the book emphasizes training supervisors to manage effectively, rather than managerial deviancy, it has a behavior modification orientation. The well-researched (at General Electric) approach presented has some aspects similar to the strategic plan presented in *Managerial Deviance*.

Robert Hershey, "Identifying the Functioning Disturbed Executive," *Personnel Journal*, May 1974, pp. 337, 349–52. A revealing article about identifying the "productive deviant."

Harry Levinson, "Alcoholism in Industry," Special Issue *Menninger Quarterly*. Available through Rutgers University—Center of Alcohol Studies, New Brunswick, N.J. 08903 (25¢). An older but useful article, still frequently quoted.

"Management Guide on Alcoholism and Other Behavioral Problems," Kemper Insurance, Long Grove, Illinois 60049. A brief guide covering the topics suggested by its title.

Manual on Alcoholism, available from Order Handling

Unit, American Medical Association, 535 North Dearborn Street, Chicago, Illinois, 60610 (50¢). Another basic reference on the topic of alcoholism.

Thomas J. Murray, "The Fight to Save Alcoholic Executives," *Dun's Review,* June 1973, pp. 72–74. A current overview of rehabilitating one form of managerial deviancy.

Lewis F. Presnall, "What About Drugs and Employees?" Public Relations Department, Kemper Insurance, Long Grove, Illinois 60049. Written by the director of rehabilitation services at Kemper, this is a brief, factual treatment of the topic.

Rachel Scott, *Muscle and Blood,* Dutton, 1974. A strong indictment of industry for subjecting workers to a variety of toxic substances in the normal conduct of their jobs. Victims, offending companies, and collaborating physicians are identified.

Kenneth A. Rouse, "What to Do About the Employee with a Drinking Problem," Public Relations, Kemper Insurance Companies, Long Grove, Illinois 60049. The late author, an acknowledged authority in the field, provides some important opinions about the identification and treatment of alcoholics.

Henry L. Tosi and W. Clay Hammer, *Organizational Behavior and Management: A Contingency Approach,* St. Clair Press, 1974. An attempt to relate the idea of environmental influence upon individuals, groups, and organizations—an orientation based on behavior modification.

Benjamin B. Wolman, *Victims of Success: Emotional Problems of Executives,* Quadrangle, New York Times, 1973. Provides some insights into the problem of personal conflicts faced by some people in managerial positions.

Notes

CHAPTER 1

1. Investigations about managerial obsolescence provide some useful information. One source is Andrew J. DuBrin, *The Practice of Managerial Psychology*, Pergamon Press, 1972, pp. 152–53. Another source is Samuel R. Connor and John S. Fielden, "Rx for Managerial Shelf Sitters," *Harvard Business Review*, November–December 1973, p. 113.

2. A recent synthesis of information in this area is Thomas J. Murray, "The Fight to Save Our Alcoholic Executives," *Dun's Review*, June 1973, pp. 72–74.

3. Two different sources of information about the recovery rate of properly treated alcoholics are consistent. According to the National Council on Alcoholism, the recovery rate has ranged between 60 and 80 percent (source: Thomas J. Murray, "The Fight to Save Our Alcoholic Executives," *Dun's Review*, June 1973, p. 73). Concerning the treatment of alcoholism, James C. Coleman notes that behavior therapy using aversion techniques yields a 50 percent rate of remission over periods as long as 10 years. Where booster treatments are given periodically, the remission rate increases to about 85 percent (source: James C. Coleman, *Abnormal Psychology and Modern Life*, 4th ed., Scott, Foresman, 1972, p. 421).

4. DuBrin, *Survival in the Sexist Jungle*, Books For Better Living, 1974, chap. 7.

5. Cited in Susan Margetts, "Pot-Smoking Young Executives," *Dun's Review*, February 1970, p. 42.

6. *Ibid.*

7. Jordan M. Scher, ed., *Drug Abuse in Industry: Growing Corporate Dilemma*, Charles C. Thomas, 1973, p. xi.

8. *Ibid.*, p. xii.

9. Quoted in Leonard Curry, "Age Bias Most Damaging Type of Discrimination," *Democrat and Chronicle*, Rochester, N.Y., June 9, 1974, p. 1C.

10. Definition quoted from a research monograph on this topic, Stanley S. Guterman, *The Machiavellians: A Social Psychological Study of Moral Character and Organization Milieu*, Univ. of Nebraska Press, 1970, p. 3.

11. Reprinted with permission from Andrew J. DuBrin, *Fundamentals of Organizational Behavior*, © 1974, Pergamon Press, Inc., p. 166.

12. Abraham Zaleznik, "Power and Politics in Organizational Life," *Harvard Business Review*, May–June 1970, p. 52.

13. The only published information I have found on this phenomenon is "Absentee Executive: AWOLism," *Newsweek*, November 17, 1969, pp. 104–106.

14. Robert F. Pearse, "The Fine Art of Managerial Hustling." Reprinted by permission of the publisher from *Personnel*, Sept./Oct. 1973.

15. *Ibid.*

16. "The FHA Scandals," *Newsweek*, May 20, 1974, pp. 87–88.

17. *Ibid.*, p. 88.

18. Mary Rita Kurycki, "Gamblers Anonymous: Trying to Win the Most Important Gamble," *Democrat and Chronicle*, Rochester, N.Y., June 30, 1974, p. 1E.

19. John M. Healy, "The Hidden Executive Vice: Gambling," *Dun's Review*, December 1973, pp. 112–15.

CHAPTER 2

1. "Alcoholism, Drug Abuse: Multi-billion Dollar Management Problems," American Management Association program flyer, November 17, 1970.

2. Susan Margetts, "Pot-Smoking Young Executives," *Dun's Review*, February 1970, p. 42.

3. Levy, "A Study of Drug-Related Criminal Behavior in Business and Industry," in Jordan M. Scher, ed., *Drug Abuse in Industry: Growing Corporate Dilemma*, Charles C. Thomas, 1973, p. 148.

4. James C. Coleman, *Abnormal Psychology and Modern Life*, 4th ed., Scott, Foresman, 1972, p. 435.

5. Parkinson, *The Law of Delay*, Houghton Mifflin, 1971.

6. Review of *The Law of Delay* in *Psychology Today*, December 1971, pp. 10, 110. Reprinted from PSYCHOLOGY TODAY Maga-

zine, December 1971. Copyright © 1971. Ziff-Davis Publishing Company. All rights reserved.

7. "Management Guide on Alcoholism and Other Behavioral Problems," Kemper Insurance, Long Grove, Ill., 60049, p. 10, n.d.

8. "Accounting: Catch-22," *Newsweek*, April 22, 1974, p. 88. Copyright © 1974, Newsweek, Inc., reprinted by permission.

9. Wyndham Robertson, "The Ten Highest-Ranking Women in Business," *Fortune*, April 1973, pp. 81–89.

10. An illuminating article about antiblack discrimination in business through 1970 is "Toiling at the Edge of the Economy," *Black Enterprise*, April 1971, pp. 65–73.

11. "Scandals: Sweatshops in the Sun," *Time*, July 30, 1973, p. 56.

12. *Ibid.*, p. 57.

13. Carr, "Can an Executive Afford a Conscience?" *Harvard Business Review*, July–August 1970, p. 63.

14. Arthur M. Louis, "The View from the Pinnacle: What Business Thinks," *Fortune*, September 1969, p. 94. Cited in a valuable source of information about business values and codes of conduct, Keith Davis and Robert L. Blomstrum, *Business, Society and Environment: Social Power and Social Response*, McGraw-Hill, 1971, chap. 9.

CHAPTER 3

1. "Clemente Promotion a Fraud?" *Democrat and Chronicle*, Rochester, N.Y., August 17, 1974, p. 3D.

2. Steiner, "What Price Success?" *Harvard Business Review*, March–April 1972, p. 70.

3. Levinson, "On Being a Middle-Aged Manager," *Harvard Business Review*, July–August 1969, p. 52. Another good source of information on this topic is William J. Constandse, "A Neglected Personnel Problem" *Personnel Journal*, February 1972, p. 131.

4. *Ibid.*

5. *Ibid.*

6. James C. Coleman, *Abnormal Psychology and Modern Life*, 4th ed., Scott, Foresman, 1972, p. 165.

7. *Ibid.*, pp. 165–68.

8. Reprinted by permission of Quadrangle/The New York Times Book Co. from *Victims of Success* by Benjamin B. Wolman, pp. 67–68. Copyright © 1973 by Benjamin B. Wolman.

9. Reprinted with permission from *Survival in the Sexist Jungle*, by Andrew J. DuBrin, copyright ©1974, Books for Better Living.

10. Wolman, *Victims of Success*, pp. 80–81.

11. An excellent overview of the influence of parent-child relationships on later development is found in Coleman, *Abnormal Psychology*, chap. 6. A tabular summary of faulty parent-child relationships is found on p. 160.

12. Guterman, *The Machiavellians: A Social Psychological Study of Moral Character and Organization Milieu*, Univ. of Nebraska Press, 1970, p. 129.

CHAPTER 4

1. Connor and Fielden, "Rx for Managerial Shelf-Sitters," *Harvard Business Review*, November–December 1973, p. 113.

2. Constandse, "A Neglected Personnel Problem," *Personnel Journal*, February 1972, p. 132.

3. *Ibid.*

4. Lester M. Cone, Jr. brought this idea to public attention, as cited in Andrew J. DuBrin, *The Practice of Managerial Psychology*, Pergamon Press, 1972, p. 149.

5. Levinson, "Who Is to Blame for the Maladaptive Manager?" *Harvard Business Review*, November–December 1965, pp. 154, 156–57.

6. Peter and Hull, *The Peter Principle: Why Things Always Go Wrong*, Morrow, 1969.

7. Most of the available research about role ambiguity and individual strain through 1972 is summarized in French and Caplan, "Organizational Stress and Individual Strain," in Alfred J. Morrow, ed., *The Failure of Success*, AMACOM, 1972, pp. 30–66.

8. *Ibid.*, p. 34.

9. *Ibid.*, pp. 34–55.

10. A further analysis of this behavior pattern is found in Robert H. Schaffer, "The Psychological Barriers to Management Effectiveness," *Business Horizons*, April 1971, p. 21.

11. French and Caplan, "Organizational Stress," p. 49.

12. Thomas J. Murray, "Peter Drucker Attacks Our Top-Heavy Corporations," *Dun's Review*, April 1971, p. 39.

13. Levinson, "Who Is to Blame?", p. 143.

14. Andrew J. DuBrin, *Fundamentals of Organizational Behavior*, Pergamon Press, 1974, p. 139.

15. An interesting analysis of the potential application of marketing principles to higher education is Eugene H. Fram, "Marketing Higher Education," in Dyckman W. Vermilye, ed., *The Future in the Making: Current Issues in Higher Education*, Jossey-Bass, 1973, pp. 56–67.

16. Cited in Clarence C. Walton, *Ethos and the Executive: Values in Managerial Making*, Prentice-Hall, 1969, p. 90.

CHAPTER 5

1. McMurry, "Clear Communications," *Harvard Business Review*, March-April, 1965, p. 133.

2. This list follows almost verbatim the information provided in "Management Guide on Alcoholism and Other Behavioral Problems," Public Relations Department, Kemper Insurance, Long Grove, Ill. 60049.

3. Scher, ed., *Drug Abuse in Industry*, Charles C. Thomas, 1973, p. 295.

4. Symptoms 1 through 6 and 9 are taken from *Ibid*. Several other items in Dr. Scher's list are more applicable to unskilled production workers.

5. Particularly relevant here is Ginott, *Between Parent and Teenager*, Macmillan, 1969; Avon Books, 1971, p. 89.

6. A helpful article about translating objectives into precise behavior is Richard K. Murray, "Behavioral Management Objectives," *Personnel Journal*, April 1973, pp. 304–306.

CHAPTER 6

1. Cited in Kenneth A. Rouse, "What to Do About the Employee with a Drinking Problem," Public Relations Department, Kemper Insurance Companies, Long Grove, Ill., p. 8.

2. Miner, *Personnel Psychology*, Macmillan, 1969, p. 238.

3. Jules Asher, "Senators Hit Mental Health Cuts," APA Monitor, Washington, D.C., September–October 1974, p. 1.

4. Carroll and Tosi, *Management by Objectives: Applications and Research*, Macmillan, 1973, p. 72. Copyright © 1973 by Macmillan Publishing Co., Inc.

5. I have synthesized additional information on the topic of counseling subordinates toward improved performance in DuBrin, *Fundamentals of Organizational Behavior*, Pergamon Press, 1974, pp. 243–56.

CHAPTER 7

1. The most exhaustive analysis of the problems of implementing behavior modification in natural settings to date is N. Dickon Repucci and J. Terry Saunders, "Social Psychology of Behavior Modification," *American Psychologist*, September 1974, pp. 649–60.

2. Readers interested in a brief overview of the essentials of rein-

forcement theory might consult David Krech, Richard S. Crutch-field, and Norman Livson, *Elements of Psychology,* 3rd ed., Knopf, 1974, Unit 16.

3. A comprehensive and technical analysis of evaluative reinforc-ers is Winfred F. Hill, "Sources of Evaluative Reinforcement," Psychological Bulletin, 1968, No. 2, pp. 132–46. Also reprinted in W.E. Scott, Jr., and L.L. Cummings, *Readings in Organizational Behavior and Human Performance,* Revised Edition, Richard D. Irwin, 1973, pp. 99–110.

4. Gupton and LeBow, "Behavior Management in a Large Indus-trial Firm," *Behavior Therapy,* 1971, no. 2, pp. 78–82.

CHAPTER 8

1. An updated review of information about the relationship be-tween child-beating by parents and juvenile delinquency is Adah Maurer, "Corporal Punishment," *American Psychologist,* August 1974, p. 624.

2. A widely read indictment of punishment in rehabilitating criminals is Karl Menninger, *The Crime of Punishment,* Viking Press, 1968.

3. McGregor's analysis has been extended by George Strauss and Leonard Sayles, *Personnel: The Human Problems of Management,* Prentice-Hall, 1972, pp. 267–68.

4. Based on information in DuBrin, *Fundamentals of Organiza-tional Behavior,* Pergamon Press, 1974, p. 260.

CHAPTER 9

1. James W. Kelley, "Case of the Alcoholic Absentee," *Harvard Business Review,* May–June 1969, p. 24.

2. Ruch and Zimbardo, *Psychology and Life,* 8th ed., Scott, Foresman, 1971, p. 631.

3. Carr, "Can an Executive Afford a Conscience?", *Harvard Business Review,* July–August 1970, p. 64.

CHAPTER 10

1. My description of pyramid sales follows that provided by "Battling the Biggest Fraud," *Time,* July 16, 1973, pp. 51–52.

2. *Ibid.,* p. 51.

3. Pearse, "The Fine Art of Managerial Hustling." Reprinted by permission of the publisher from *Personnel,* Sept./Oct. 1973, p. 55.

4. Hershey, "Identifying the Functioning Disturbed Executive," *Personnel Journal,* May 1974, p. 350.

CHAPTER 11

1. My analysis of shortcomings in peer ratings follows that presented by John B. Miner, *Personnel Psychology*, Macmillan, 1969, p. 86.

2. *Ibid.*, p. 87.

3. Hershey, "Identifying the Functioning Disturbed Executive *Personnel Journal*, May 1974, p. 352.

4. *Ibid.*

5. The information presented follows closely an analysis found in "The Whistle Blowers," *Time*, April 17, 1972, pp. 85–86. Reprinted by permission from TIME, The Weekly Newsmagazine; Copyright Time Inc.

6. *Ibid.*, p. 86.

7. *Ibid.*, p. 85.

8. *Ibid.*, p. 86.

CHAPTER 12

1. Harry Levinson, "Asinine Attitudes Toward Motivation," *Harvard Business Review*, January–February 1973, p. 73. Levinson's book. *The Great Jackass Fallacy*, Harvard Business School, 1973, contains the same information plus a related group of essays.

2. Arnold P. Goldstein and Melvin Sorcher, *Changing Supervisor Behavior*, Pergamon Press, 1974.

3. Reprinted from the December 18, 1971 issue of *Business Week* by special permission. © 1971 by McGraw-Hill, Inc.

4. *APA Monitor*, June 1974, p. 3.

5. Marvin Karlins and Lewis M. Andrews, *Psychology: What's in It for Us?*, Random House, 1973, p. 109.

6. This case history is taken verbatim, with the exclusion of the names of a few locations, from Sharland Trotter, "ACLU Scores Token Economy," *APA Monitor*, August 1974, pp. 1 and 7.

7. Skinner and Cline are both cited in John R. Murphy, "Is It Skinner or Nothing?" *Training and Development Journal*, February 1972, p. 3. Skinner is not referenced, but see John Cline, "Learning COD—Can the Schools Buy Success? *Saturday Review*, September 18, 1971.

Index